BUBBLE WRAPPED CHILDREN

BUBBLE WRAPPED CHILDREN

First Published in 2012
© Copyright Helen Oakwater

A CIP catalogue record for this book is available from the British Library
ISBN Paperback 9781780920979
ISBN ePub is 9781780920986
ISBN PDF is 9781780920993

Published by MX Publishing
335 Princess Park Manor,
Royal Drive, London N11 3GX
www.mxpublishing.co.uk

Cover design by Johanna Gale

Cover compiled by www.staunch.com

BUBBLE

WRAPPED

CHILDREN

How social networking is transforming
the face of 21st century adoption

HELEN OAKWATER

ACKNOWLEDGMENTS

Until I started writing I never read the acknowledgments in books. I do now, because although writing is a staggeringly solitary activity and the content has come from my head, heart and gut; others have implanted ideas, questions, thoughts and fresh perspectives. Professional and personal support has come from unexpected quarters during the writing of this book and in preceding decades.

I have grouped people for ease of reference; their order is not significant. There are others not mentioned here who have aided my journey with a word, phrase or action. Also let's be real, some have contributed to my learnings through their actions which deliberately or inadvertently caused me pain. Others astonished me with their naivety, ignorance or inappropriate comments. Sometimes fury at the system taught me a lesson. I have attended numerous training courses, read many books and had conversations with hundreds of people. All moulded my thinking and I'm grateful. Rather like a vegetable soup, once blended they are impossible to separate, however some special pieces have been kept back as a garnish.

Adoption World
Without Adoption UK my head would have exploded. I phoned the help line one day in 1997 and said, "My ten-year-old stole my purse last weekend and my credit card holder this weekend and no one, including my husband, believes me." There was a roar of laughter at the end of the phone and Philly Morrall said, "Well I do." A weight lifted from my shoulders instantly. That support has been offered to adopters for 40 years. A huge thank you to Hilary Chambers, Philly Morrall and Jonathan Pearce, the CEOs during those 40 years, and all the staff, trustees and volunteers in Adoption UK who offer a unique lifeline and support to adopters.

To all the adopters and foster carers with whom I have shared stories, laughter, wisdom, strategies and sympathy: I am indebted. Many have generously permitted me to share their stories within the text. Thank you. Others have assisted in the writing of this book; a few need spotlighting. Karam Ranwan, the editor of the Adoption Today magazine who encouraged me to write articles and find my voice while Jonathan Pearce's structural and content feedback sharpened the text. Jenny Elliott, my first social worker and walking evidence that there are some outstanding professionals in the field of Social Work who, even though it wasn't her job, over two decades re-entered our lives whenever we screamed for help; a professional who became a friend. Thank you all.

I'm also indebted to Felicity Collier, former CEO of BAAF (British Association for Adoption and Fostering) whom I first met in a BBC radio studio. She took me under her wing, put me on a platform which resulted in an invitation to join the Government Task Force which then deepened my learning of the issues facing Local Authorities and we shared many delightful long train journeys. More recently, Craig Wilkinson in BAAF Wales has encouraged me to speak from the heart and tell it like it is. Thanks mate.

The therapy and wisdom Family Futures shared with my family was transformational. Alan Burnell, Jay Vaughan and Christine Gordon demonstrated their characteristic courage both forming the organisation and in the interventions we experienced. Several years later my learning from the two-year Attachment and Adoption postgraduate course helped shape this book, while Alan's contribution to my thinking on contact and the need for inoculation was profound.

Lynda Gilbert has been my mentor and friend for a long time. She has been there through the really, really tough times; a lighthouse for sanity when the only choice was a rock or a hard place. Her wisdom, humour and insights have helped me and many, many others. Her quiet, sensible contributions at national level for many years as Adoption UK's policy advisor have influenced thinking at the highest level. An unsung hero in the adoption world, Lynda is always stimulating, great fun to be with and a rare six on the Empathy scale. Thank you my friend.

NLP (Neuro Linguistic Programming)
While Adoption UK stopped my head exploding, NLP made sense of the nonsense. It showed specifically how my children's behaviour was simply an expression of their inner world. NLP offered solutions, models, transformational tools and hope. Ian McDermott, my first teacher, demonstrated a gentle way of delivering training and being. Robert Dilts offered sponsorship, encouragement and authenticity while Judy DeLozier demonstrated an exquisite sparkly coaching style which I'm striving to emulate. My friend Suzi Smith taught me sub-modalities, the benefits of singing in training sessions, trauma cures and the joy of sisterhood. Art Giser's incorporation of energetic perspectives into NLP has transformed my life and body. Michael Grinders teaching on Group Dynamics and Non Verbal Behaviour accompanied by his wonderful way of being, provided me with yet more support and strategies to manage difficult behaviour. Thank you, mentors one and all.

Even though I entered the NLP world purely for my own benefit and self development, I slid into coaching career, where I learned trauma can be dissolved and beliefs updated. Clients showed me that courage takes many forms, humour is always useful, breaking icons is fun, compassion essential and healing possible. To my fabulous clients, who must remain nameless, witnessing your healing increased my knowledge about the effects of child maltreatment. Thank you so much.

Book Specific
My thanks to book coach Jackie Lofthouse who helped me feel the fear and do it anyway, to Steve Emecz and the team at MX Publishing who with grace and speed physically made it happen. I've had a terrific team of peer reviewers who have sharpened up sloppy writing, suggested additional content, uttered encouraging noises and constructive criticisms. So Ruth Adams, Pauline Crawford, Annabel Fisher, Olive Hickmott, Angela Horne, Jonathan Pearce and Craig Wilkinson thank you for your feedback. All mistakes and errors are mine.

Closer to home
Friends have offered encouragement and tolerated my head down single-minded approach to writing. Maybe now I can get out more! One group needs a special mention. The EXPECT group who meet bi-monthly, exchange and share professional insights, including some of the models used in this book. So my thanks go to Sylvana Caloni, Morgan Chambers, Margot Corbin, Jeanette Cowley, Cynthia Haddock, Charmian Ingham and Terri McNerney; models of excellence themselves.

Obviously I want to thank my children without whom none of this would be possible. You have each given me very different experiences of being a mother. My life was transformed that Tuesday you moved into my house and it became our home. Much water has passed under the bridge since then and will continue to do so. I love you and thank you.

CONTENTS

BUBBLE WRAPPED CHILDREN

INTRODUCTION AND PERSONAL PRE-FRAME

This book was not planned; it simply demanded to be written. Others encouraged me to voice the unspeakable, the shadow side of adoption and dispel the "happy ever after" illusion by highlighting the needs of maltreated children and those who parent them.

"Getting" trauma

After two decades in the adoption world I have realised it's quite simple. Until you or anyone else "gets trauma", i.e. really understands and appreciates the lasting damage trauma does to a child, you don't "get" the need for adoption support and therapeutic reparenting. My intent in this book is to help readers "get trauma" and understand its impact on children, because it's the key to transformational thinking and making adoption work long term. When people "get trauma" their focus, behaviour and decisions change, it's the light bulb moment. This applies to government ministers, parents, social care, mental health and education professionals.

Since the end of the 20th Century when Prime Minister Tony Blair spotlighted adoption, I have watched and listened to government minister after minister make changes in adoption: some good, others less useful. None "got trauma". The Adoption Bill in 2002 gave adopters a right to an assessment for adoption support, but, ludicrously, no right to that support. Yes, we've diagnosed your thirst, but won't give you a drink. As we are now on the verge of another wave of government-led modifications to adoption, I hope this book will be a useful tool in the forthcoming discussions and political lobbying.

Why now?

In 2010 a number of my friends, colleagues and acquaintances in the adoption world suddenly experienced their adopted children being reconnected to their birth family via Facebook. Me too. My children received an unexpected email via Facebook from a birth parent just days before Christmas 2009.

My reaction was the same as other adoptive parents, a rollercoaster of intense emotions in tandem with a desire to be strong and supportive for my children. The repeated phrase I've heard from adoptive parents is "it feels like a slow motion car crash". I concur. Battering and bruising, yet you hold onto the wheel and try to steer to a safe place; simultaneously experiencing your own upheaval while watching and trying to assist in your child's turmoil. Yes it's messy.

BUBBLE WRAPPED CHILDREN

After my initial horror at the devastation social networking brought to adoption families, I now believe it could be the catalyst for positive transformation, but only if decision makers "get trauma" and the long-term effects of child maltreatment. Adoption planning must embrace this truth. Although not formally structured in this way, what the book offers is partially a SWOT Analysis (Strengths, Weaknesses, Opportunities and Threats) of adoption today.

Why me?

Despite being an adoptive parent for two decades and for big chunks of that time holding professional roles in the adoption world, I was rocked by the events that occurred within my own family. It threw me off course for many months and had far-reaching personal consequences. I say this simply so that adopters in a similar position will not feel they are alone when their reactions overwhelm and surprise them.

For a number of years I've contributed articles to the Adoption UK magazine including two during the spring 2010 highlighting the impact of Facebook on adoption. In December 2010, I released the eBook, Facebook: Adoption Destabilizer. This led to speaking at conferences, delivering training, media interviews, conversations and unsolicited emails from adopters telling me their sad stories. I was witnessing a totally unexpected factor explode in the adoption world; its shrapnel takes many forms and is still landing.

My credentials for writing this book include:
- Δ being an experienced adoptive parent of three children,
- Δ several years attachment based therapy with children at Family Futures
- Δ former membership of two local authority adoption panels
- Δ former membership of the government's Adoption and Permanence Task Force.
- Δ various roles within the charity Adoption UK including two terms as a trustee
- Δ two-year part-time postgraduate course in Attachment and Adoption with Family Futures
- Δ ten years teaching in secondary schools
- Δ being an NLP (Neuro-Linguistic Programming) coach and trainer

In parallel with the learnings gleaned from parenting my own children, my personal growth path was enhanced by NLP. From my first day on a Neuro-Linguistic Programming training course, in 2002, my world changed for the better. NLP offered models, principles and a style of thinking which empowered me and explained my children's behaviour. NLP subtlety pervades this book. NLP is based on modelling excellence, pattern detection, rapport, sensory acuity, noticing differences, behavioural flexibility and focuses on well-formed outcomes. My experience with coaching clients has shown me that much trauma can be released and converted into empowering learnings. My intent is to bring hope, insight and some transformational tools into the adoption world.

Metaphors, models and pictures

Metaphors are frequently used in NLP; they are processed in the right brain and unconscious mind which enable you to receive a message or learning from a "non-telling" route, similar to parables, fables and fairy stories. Metaphors are used throughout the book; the title "Bubble Wrapped Children" conjures an image in your mind.

Throughout the book I offer some specific established models used in psychology, business and the 'self-help' world. These combined with the new scientific advances in brain mapping offer new ways to better understand maltreated children and their abusers. Even though models are useful because they are visual, logical and give a framework for thinking, it doesn't make them 'right'. However it does assist in encouraging reflective practice, alternative ways of looking at a situation and can provide valuable calibration tools.

One picture is worth a thousand words; or as my mentor Michael Grinder would say "Go Visual". I have. Graphics litter the text, visual language is heard throughout and I also hope to provoke emotional responses. My proudest moments as a member of the Adoption Task Force occurred after I delivered a very brief presentation to local councillors. One confessed; "I don't mind admitting, that woman made me cry."

"I've learned that people will forget what you said, people will forget what you did,
but people will never forget how you made them feel."
Maya Angelou

Yes, I want you to feel while reading this book, to laugh, maybe cry, get angry but be touched, deeply touched; because adoption, child maltreatment and trauma are about living, breathing people; it's not an academic exercise, it really, really matters. Oh, and I use quotes a lot too.

Metaphors and book structure

The book structure keeps at its core the most important thing: the child. The child should always be at the centre of any care planning, parenting strategies and decision making.

BUBBLE WRAPPED CHILDREN

The child is at the heart of this book which roughly follows the child's path as he ages and gets taller, yes ages and gets taller, because the word "matures" is not appropriate for traumatised children. Fortunately for most children their ageing and maturation go hand in hand. Rather like a small river heading towards the sea, their life starts gently flowing, initially narrow and shallow, then widening, deepening yet fundamentally running in the same direction with occasional eddies, rocks and whirlpools. As the child approaches the open waters of the sea and adulthood, the now wider river is affected by the sea tide hence there is some in and out, undulating flow, a metaphor for the turbulent, often muddy waters of adolescence.

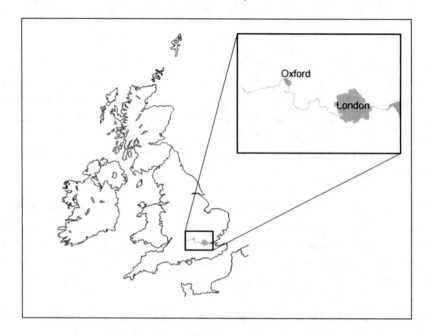

For a maltreated child it is different. Their river is more like the Thames, the longest river in England with over twenty tributaries, frequent backwaters and a meandering path that takes in numerous bridges, islands, and some tunnels. On the outskirts of west London at Teddington Lock its character changes dramatically. It becomes tidal, flowing in and out, twice daily. The tidal Thames is like adolescence for traumatised children, it keeps going up and down, backwards and forwards at a rapid rate, with massive changes in height of between five and seven metres over twelve hours. Teddington Lock is metaphorically the start of adolescence. The Thames flowing through bustling London gets deeper, muddier and frequently changes direction, the volume of water immense. Eventually it reaches the wide expanses of the Thames Estuary, which despite feeling like the sea, is still part of the river. The sea is still miles downstream.

4

I hope this lengthy Thames metaphor will stop some of the "all children do that" attitude which ignorant adults bring to the subject of adoption. Yes, if all child development and parenting is like a river. Which one do you want to navigate, sail or swim down? Which are the easy ones and which the biggest challenge? What would you need for that journey?

Maltreated children have many extra components and challenges in their lives. Mucky tributaries adding to the complex flow of their lives. These complexities and contributory factors are reflected in the books' structure, which is intended as a map and travel guide for each readers own unique journey. There are certain fixed points linked to children's development stages and offshoots related to parenting which warrant deeper exploration. Just like navigating the Thames, you can picnic in Oxford, pause for tea at historic Windsor Castle, at Westminster get the big global picture aboard the London Eye or indulge in candy floss on Southend Pier. In the final section we set sail into the uncharted waters of future adoption practices, mindful of reefs, wrecks, undercurrents and squalls and suggest where some navigation buoys must be placed and preventative lighthouses built.

Boundaries
Readers will find some topics shallower than others. Bubble Wrapped Children concentrates primarily on children's needs, the birth parent perspective and wider ramifications of Facebook intrusions. Although the adopter's perspective and parenting traumatised children each have a separate chapter these are explored in greater depth further in "Making Sense of Nonsense", the book I was writing before social networking exploded into adoption in 2010. The adolescent adoptee perspective not included as a specific component in Bubble Wrapped Children, simply because it's too early to draw any meaningful conclusions from ongoing events and recent reconnections.

My intent with both books is to shine a light into some of the dark, unlabelled places which exist in the world of adoption and fostering world and for children neglected and abused in their infancy. Both books place the reader into the shoes of each player, to gain insight into their world, their perspective and challenges. With this knowledge decision makers and professionals will hopefully be empowered to make robust decisions quickly.

> *"The greatest gift we can offer each other is the framework*
> *in which to think for ourselves"*
> Nancy Kline

Housekeeping

All the anecdotes and stories in the book have been anonymized by changing key identifying features and I am deeply grateful to those who generously shared their experiences. My children lead independent lives and do not share my surname, so their identity is protected.

I have used he/she/they to refer to individuals as seemed appropriate, to create an easy read. No deliberate political correctness or gender balancing. Similarly simple neutral names are used so readers can create a child in their mind's eye.

Because adoption is my primary knowledge base I have kept the book inside the adoption arena even though many of the issues raised and recommendations apply equally to children in foster care. Children in long term foster care often have complex, ongoing contact arrangements with their birth family. Bubble Wrapped Children does not tackle them.

Within this book I have taken a multidisciplinary approach, sourcing and referred to material from many others; accrediting them each time for two reasons. Firstly honouring the sources sits comfortably with my values of integrity and honesty. Secondly some readers will want to return to the original texts for further information.

Please consider the content of this book as pieces of a jigsaw which you can add to your existing picture and framework. Chapter Zero provides the framework for unfolding the issues, the edges of the puzzle. My starting point in Chapter 1 is where the spotlight should always be focused, on the child. What happens to a child before s/he is adopted.

This book is the map, not the territory. I hope your journey is enlightening, your inner landscape is transformed and as a result of reading Bubble Wrapped Children you will contribute your small piece to the transformation of adoption.

"Never doubt that a small group of thoughtful committed citizens can change the world. Indeed, it's the only thing that ever has."
Margaret Mead

Take Good Care

Helen Oakwater

London
November 2011

CHAPTER ZERO

If you think adopted children are safe from an approach by the birth family they were removed from, think again. Social networking has blown that protection sky high.

Facebook allows you to search for anyone and email anyone. Anyone you know, anyone you want to know, anyone you once knew or complete strangers. Present, past and future connections can be made via the web. Relationships can be formed or rekindled. Identities can be faked, lies told, history rewritten.

Adopted children are being connected to their birth families via Facebook. Some children have actively searched for birth family members; others simply received an email in their Facebook inbox which explodes in their face.

Hello, I am your father. I have been searching for you ever since you were stolen by social services. You look beautiful. I love you so much.

darlin son i am so hapy coz iv found u ere I bin lokin for ages plse rit bak coz uv bin told lies bout me i always luved u n nevr stopd thinkin bout u b gr8 2 c u.

Messages like these, some in normal English, some in 'text speak', are retraumatising adopted children. Adoptive families are being blown apart. Several adopted children have left their adoptive parents and moved back in with their birth parents, sometimes within days of reconnecting. Other teenage adoptees have been completely thrown by the unwanted contact, their schooling, relationships and mental health have suffered. Some did not sit exams, others dropped out of college or university because they were so destabilised.

The two emails above might look innocuous. However the birth father in the first is a known paedophile. The second is a mother who had six children removed by social services due to her alcohol abuse, chaotic lifestyle and her lack of empathy. She simply could not see the pain she inflicted on a succession of children and the damage done to them. Her circumstances and attitude have hardly changed since the children were removed yet she still grieves for them.

In one case, the birth parent reconnected easily because the child was a "Facebook friend" to a member of an old foster family. In the other example the birth parent simply typed in the child's first names and their date of birth then trawled through the photographs displayed on Facebook.

BUBBLE WRAPPED CHILDREN

Children can legally register on Facebook at thirteen. Teenagers now access the internet via their mobile phones – not just computers – so it is impossible for parents to monitor or control. You can have several Facebook accounts. Curiosity will motivate searching. It always has and always will.

So far many of the reconnections via Facebook have caused much confusion, pain and sorrow, because they have been built on lies, delusions and false hope. The participants, whether willing or shocked, have been unprepared and unsupported. Preparation and support are the keys to successful post-adoption contact, whatever form it takes.

Instant connection
Until a few years ago post adoption reunions were initiated by an adult, sometimes using an intermediary service which offered counselling and approached all involved with sensitivity and respect. Now, technology allows reconnection within hours of searching. There is no time to reflect, no mediation, no safeguards or supervision. Whoever makes the first move, the other person's circumstances and situation are completely unknown. Is this a good time? Do they have mental health issues, exams, drug problems? Have they just split from a long relationship? What support do they have? How will those around them feel about this contact? How fragile and vulnerable are each of the parties involved? How will the adoptive parents feel and react? Will they even know? What will happen afterwards?

Reasons for adoption: now and then
Celebrity adoptees share joyful reunion stories and promote adoption. Recently there has been a spurt of TV programmes and articles where adult adoptees in their 40s, 50s and 60s have been reunited with their birth mothers, fathers or siblings. There is a public and media appetite for these 'feel good' adoption stories, where often an underlying message is that blood is thicker than water. The honeymoon period is public, but the long-term outcomes undisclosed. This reinforces the public notion that adoption equals relinquished babies, whereas for the last few decades adoption occurs because the state intervened and removed a maltreated child from his toxic parents. Subsequently a judge, after examining copious evidence, agrees with the Social Service's recommendation that the birth parents do not have the capability, or the future capacity, to learn how to parent this child adequately. These parents did not "give up" their child: he was forcibly removed because their parenting style was abusive, neglectful or deeply inadequate. Chapter 4 details some measurable skills, characteristics and traits including empathy, emotional intelligence and executive functioning thinking skills whose absences inhibit their parenting capacity. These models also serve as useful analytical tools for professionals.

Maltreatment, wiring, trauma and bubble wrap

What is the consequence of infant maltreatment? What imprints do abuse, neglect and chaos leave on a child? Great technological leaps this century offer evidence which support older anecdotal findings.

Thanks to the advent of brain imaging, we know that neurons which fire together wire together. So a child raised in a calm, secure yet stimulating setting will have a brain wired differently to that of a child deprived of maternal care living in a chaotic, scary environment. An infant's brain forms thousands of new neural connections every second. More are formed in the first year of life than at any subsequent time. We also know the brain is 'plastic' and in the right circumstances parts can be 'rewired'.

Another scientific and technological leap within this century is our knowledge of brain functioning which offers hope for healing trauma. Awareness of Post Traumatic Stress Disorder has grown, mainly due to affected soldiers returning from war zones receiving sympathetic media and movie coverage. The symptoms listed include flashbacks, sleep difficulties, anger outbursts and a general 'dysfunctionality'.

The impact of trauma on the adult brain is recognised, however the impact of trauma on child's developing brain is not widely acknowledged, tricky to classify yet profound. The superb research, including brain scanning, undertaken by Dr Bruce Perry at the Child Trauma Academy unarguably proves that maltreatment inhibits normal infant brain development. In Chapter 8 the proposed DSM classification of Developmental Trauma Disorder is explained and by integrating this with Chapter 2, how children's needs change with time, readers can get a deeper understanding of the impact of early trauma on children and its disturbing legacy.

Many adopted children suffered terribly before placement. Their world was terrifying, chaotic, unpredictable; an unsafe place where adults could not be trusted or failed to shield you from harm. These children protected themselves by hiding their true feelings, shutting down emotionally, being compliant or aggressive or both. Their observable behaviour often seems to makes no sense. Metaphorically they wrapped themselves in bubble wrap for safety, a fantastic protection strategy; but it warps their view of the world and it distorts our view of them. Gently removing the bubble wrap, layer by layer, is the complex task adoptive parents face for many years, including during adolescence.

BUBBLE WRAPPED CHILDREN

Adolescence

Teenager rebel; it's part of their job description. They experiment with their identity, habits, clothing and relationships. Secrecy is normal. They often reject many of their parent's values, creating conflict and confrontation. Some behaviour is due to the changing brain chemistry and hormone fluctuations; adolescence is both a physical and psychological passage.

During adolescence the brain has a burst of activity and fresh growth, so the potential to rewire and prune existing circuits is huge. It is a fantastic healing opportunity for adopted children, particularly those who received appropriate therapy and support in middle childhood. Unexpected contact via Facebook can, and does, severely sabotaged this healing opportunity, because the child becomes retraumatized.

All the family r lookin forward to seeing u at cousin veronicas wedding next week. We will meet you off the train and have a great party.

That message was posted publicly on the Facebook page of Ann, an adopted teenager. All her virtual and real 'friends' read the comment, leading to difficult questions at school, forcing the disclosure that she had 'another family' and her squirming at the insensitive, yet common, question 'why did they give you up?' Fortunately she tearfully confessed to her adoptive parents about the wedding reunion plan, which involved a 250-mile train journey for a party with the entire birth family including those who had abused her. Her adoptive parents are picking up the pieces from that incident and now understand that the regular interactions with her birth parents and siblings caused Ann to be particularly uptight and aggressive. For several months Ann's healing was suspended because her birth family were 'in her face' and retraumatising her.

Birth families offer an escape route for a vulnerable rebellious teenage adoptee who is frequently in conflict with his boundary-holding adoptive parents. They encourage cooperative, considerate behaviour, schooling and responsible living. Birth families offer something different, which is far more alluring and also feel strangely familiar

Processing the past: the body keep score

Trauma is stored within the body; sensory memories are held at a cellular level. As trauma expert Bessel Van Der Kolk MD, director of the Trauma Center in Boston nutshells, "the body keeps score". Maltreated children have sensory triggers that reconnect them to unconscious memories from their brutal past. That's why for many adopted children linking to their birth family stirs up old, oddly recognisable sensations, plus a high voltage cocktail of positive and negative emotions.

By learning what happened to them in their early life, children can begin making sense of their inner world. Robust life story work which deals with the gruesome facts, not just the nice stuff, is crucial and will protect them during adolescence and in later life. Appropriate therapy to process the trauma associated with maltreatment is essential. Ongoing, facilitated, direct contact may be the vaccine which protects them from future contamination via social networking.

Looking beyond now and towards the 2020s, we know adopted children will be able to reconnect to their birth family well before adulthood. These children will benefit hugely if they are more resilient and knowledgeable about themselves. The adoption world must change some existing practices and introduce therapeutic work in mid-childhood or earlier. Waiting until inevitable problems explode in adolescence is daft and not cost-effective. Brain plasticity makes early intervention strategies a no-brainer for both child protection and therapeutic interventions.

Contact

Contact in adoption has always been a complex issue. The reasons underlying searching and reconnection need addressing. Facebook is just the search engine, the root causes include grief, loss, identity issues, teenage rebellion, curiosity and to make sense of ourselves. Big, emotionally charged stuff. When is contact good; what circumstances make it 'bad'? How can it be most effective? Should it be face-to-face or via a third-party letterbox? Should it change with time? One of the biggest and most difficult questions "What does contact do?" has numerous answers, varied opinions and conflicting research. That question pervades the book with a dedicated chapter focusing on the purpose, structure and outcomes of high quality contact.

Even though direct face-to-face contact between a child and the birth parents is currently unusual; ongoing, indirect 'letterbox contact' via a third party is often set up. This may be an exchange of letters and photos once or twice a year. Sometimes it is just one way, the adoptive family share information and photos about the child with specified members of the birth family. It is monitored and safe. However some birth parents have scanned pictures and placed them on their Facebook pages; occasionally with a request to "help me find my little princess".

One feature worth noting is the viral nature of many of these reconnections. Within days of the first message, text or call, adopted children are linked to siblings, aunts, grandparents, uncles and birth parents and their new partners, often inundated with messages, requests and guilt-laden emotional outpourings. Anecdotal evidence is that teenagers tell their adoptive parents months after the metaphorical horse has bolted and the stable door is swinging, sadly. However, by then, there's lots of manure around.

BUBBLE WRAPPED CHILDREN

Things will never be the same again

Social networking and technological advances will fundamentally change the shape of adoption and particularly contact. Because the issues raised are unique to this decade and only surfaced in 2009, radical rethinking is required. Knowing that with just one click, unsupervised direct contact between adopted teenagers and their birth family could happen via Facebook, the adoption world must review its current and future practices to pre-empt the issue and implement damage limitation strategies.

Technology is galloping ahead; imagine combining face recognition software with a programme that predicts how a toddler will look at seventeen, throw in geographic location data and after a few hours on the web an individual is 'found'. The choice then is whether to connect honestly, stalk, monitor, ignore or link using an alias.

Facebook was only launched in 2004, yet now has a membership equivalent to the fourth largest country in the world. Most people, especially teenagers and young people, obtain their information via the internet. The world has shrunk; hyperlinks, clever algorithms, instant connections and digital technology transform our behaviour. Adoption practices must adapt to accommodate the constant technological advances and the changing needs of adoptive families by tackling root causes not symptoms.

Adoption is being transformed by social networking and it's unstoppable. Will the changes be healthy and positive or hurtful and destructive for those affected? This book seeks to address that dilemma and answer the 'why', 'what' 'how' and 'what if' questions. There are useful theoretical models offering new perspectives, plus fresh insights, solutions and practical ideas for parents and professionals.

Threat or Opportunity?

If all those involved in adoption face up to the reality and ramifications of contact via social networking we can harness the learnings and transform the impact of Facebook on adoption from a threat into an opportunity. However, without radical changes in adoption support and a massive increase in the availability of decent therapeutic interventions, social networking could destroy thousands of existing adoptive placements while current and future prospective adopters are being set up to fail.

Yes, it really is that dramatic; yes, it really is a crisis; and yes, in conjunction with other proposed changes in the adoption world it is a fantastic opportunity to transform adoption and heal maltreated children – but only if we all have the courage to face up to what is beneath the bubble wrap.

PART 1: PRE-ADOPTION ISSUES

Imagination is more important than knowledge"
Albert Einstein

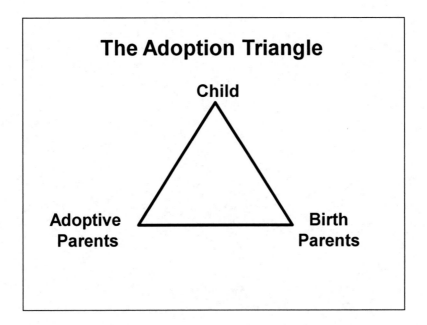

"Wounds that can't be seen are more painful than those that can be seen and healed by a doctor."
Nelson Mandela

CHAPTER ONE

WHAT HAPPENS BEFORE A CHILD IS PLACED
FOR ADOPTION?

Children placed for adoption are unique because their legal relationship with their birth family was severed by the state. The children central to this book are those who have been removed from their birth families by Social Services, against their parents' wishes. There was serious concern for the child's welfare because their birth parents could not keep them safe and nurtured. For a range of reasons, explored later, these parents consistently failed the child. Although it does happen, nowadays it is rare for a child to be relinquished at birth.

Currently less than 5% of children within the care system are placed for adoption. This may, to some readers, appear a very small number, but many children within the care system are older, have continuing links with their birth family or may be in care for short periods. Government statistics tell us that 54% entered the care system in 2010/11 because of abuse or neglect. In March 2011 there were 65,520 Looked After Children in England, of whom 74% were in foster care.

There are many families who benefit and learn much from the support and assistance of social workers, enabling them to parent their children better and keep them within the family. Sometimes Social Services involvement is ongoing, with children staying in foster care for weeks, months or years. Most return to their birth parents completely or for big chunks of time during which they have regular contact with their birth families. Sometimes respite care is used at short regular periods to give the family a break.

In an ideal world all parents would be good parents; in the real world most parents are, to coin Winnicott's phrase, 'good enough', while some are inadequate, a few are toxic. It's the role of Social Services to detect the inadequate and toxic parents, and provide support, education, supervision while frequently assessing the adults. Determining whether these adults have the capacity to change is part of the social worker's role. This is a tricky business which can take considerable time. Fortunately many parents are able to step up and learn how to be better parents. However a few are not: their children are being maltreated and suffering, with no likelihood of change in the foreseeable future. The longer they stay with their birth families, the greater the damage. These children need to be removed quickly.

BUBBLE WRAPPED CHILDREN

Deciding that a child should be removed from their birth family is a difficult decision for all involved. The fundamental role of Social Services is to support families and keep them together. An individual social worker may have invested much time, energy and effort in keeping a family together, so to recommend the removal of the child can for some feel like a personal failure. This is compounded by the huge case loads faced by all social workers in under-resourced departments. This results in drift and delay for many children for whom there was insufficient time to map out the child's inner landscape and everyday life experience. Like others, I have sometimes witnessed dreadful social work practice which stemmed from ignorance, over-optimism, inadequate training, and poor supervision. Blaming individuals is inappropriate and pointless; the system needs transforming. Excellence does exist; it can be modelled and replicated.

> *"I look around the world and see excellence and I want to share it"*
> John Grinder

The decision making process in adoption

In essence the local authority recommends that, based on the evidence they have assembled, a child should be adopted because their birth family are unable to parent them to an acceptable level. This evidence, plus further reports are presented at court where the judge decides whether or not the child should be placed for adoption. Sounds simple in principle; however, the devil is in the detail. The process is complex; evidence is acquired from historical data, psychological assessments, expert witnesses, medical advice etc. Various reports are written, scrutinised internally and subsequently reviewed by the local authority adoption panel, an independent group with wide-ranging adoption experience who "support, defer or disagree" with the "best interest is adoption" recommendation. All these papers and reports, the size and weight of several phone books, form part of the court proceedings.

Our court system is adversarial rather than inquisitorial: the intent in the criminal court being to establish proof "beyond reasonable doubt", while in the civil court, where adoption cases are heard, it is to determine "the balance of probabilities". It is a binary decision; the battle is to beat the other side, which makes adoption proceedings lengthy. On the one hand you have the local authority wanting to remove all parental responsibility from the birth parents, on the other hand the birth parents who don't want to lose their child. The judge considers the evidence from children's guardians and CAFCASS officers plus both sides' legal arguments before making a decision. However, proceedings are often adjourned and delayed as one side disputes an expert's report (often psychological assessments) and requests yet another report from a different expert. This often takes months, so yet more drift and delay for the child who has already spent months or even years in foster care which can compound the damage already done.

Why are children removed from their birth families and subsequently adopted? What evidence is required? What has happened to them?

Overarching principles and reasons for child's removal
Parents who consistently and repeatedly fail to meet their child's needs and are unable to put the child's needs ahead of their own, now or in the foreseeable future are at risk of having their children removed by the local authority.

When the child is initially removed, Social Services must state the reason for removal. Although frequently only one category of maltreatment may be listed, it is often a combination of factors. The maltreatment categories below are taken from "Working Together to Safeguard Children", published in 2010 by HM Government, DCFS.

"Sexual abuse involves forcing or enticing a child or young person to take part in sexual activities, not necessarily involving a high level of violence, whether or not the child is aware of what is happening.

Emotional abuse is the persistent emotional maltreatment of a child such as to cause severe and persistent adverse effects on the child's emotional development.

Physical abuse may involve hitting, shaking, throwing, poisoning, burning or scalding, drowning, suffocating, or otherwise causing physical harm to a child. Physical harm may also be caused when a parent or carer fabricates the symptoms of, or deliberately induces, illness in a child.

Neglect is the persistent failure to meet a child's basic physical and/or psychological needs, likely to result in the serious impairment of the child's health or development. Neglect may occur during pregnancy as a result of maternal substance abuse."

The chart gives specific examples of reasons children are permanently removed from their birth families due to maltreatment, the possible impact on the child and suggestions for the beliefs children may then form about the world and themselves.

Classification	What was done to them Some examples & experiences	What it did to them The child's interpretations & possible beliefs formed
Emotional Abuse	Berated, insulted, compared unfavourably to others, ignored	*I am wrong, bad, worthless.* They want me dead. *I should not be alive, I'm not wanted*
Physical Abuse	Beaten, thrashed, burned, used as ashtray, hit with chair/stick/hand/belt, locked in cupboard	The world is a dangerous place, *I am bad & powerless,*
Sexual Abuse	Violated, raped, forced to watch or participate in sexual acts	Destroyed innocence. *I can't trust anyone*
Neglect	Unfed for days, nappies not changed, no toys, no interaction with adults, left alone for hours, unwashed, no play	No self concept. *I don't matter, life is hopeless, I am helpless &/or rage filled.* *Do I even exist?*
Chaotic environment	Lots of different carers, locations, broken promises, frequent moves, squalor	No safe or secure base. *I am terrified.*
Trauma	A combination of events and experiences that felt life threatening or overwhelming to the child	*I am going to die.* *I must disappear*

This chart demonstrates some of the difficulties of defining child maltreatment and its subsequent effect. Often you can't tell for years the true and lasting impact of the maltreatment on an individual child and the only person who really knows what the child experienced is the child himself. Professionals will see snapshots of the child's life, but will not see or know the entire story. Only the child records a full sensory movie film of every waking moment while the professionals have the equivalent of occasional single still frames of the film from which to assess and make sense of the child's life. The same is true for us all; we are the only people who know exactly what happened to us and how we have made sense of those experiences. You are the expert on you, your life experiences, how you felt at the time and how you feel about them now.

Neglect

We know that 70% of children placed for adoption were removed because of known abuse or neglect. Please note the significance of the word "known". One extra point is worth flagging here. The category of 'neglect' is sometimes difficult to prove, causing debates and disagreements, particularly in court where judges want concrete evidence. This can contribute to delays in decision making. If we consider neglect through a child's eyes it may be a useful reframe. Hunger involves a physical and emotional experience, and in extremis the feeling you might die. Physical sores from unchanged nappies could be viewed as physical abuse; ignoring and not talking to an infant is emotionally painful. To some neglect may sound a weaker, less damaging category than abuse, yet the opposite is true. Think back to the Romanian orphans.

"If you have to choose between abuse and neglect; choose abuse, it does less damage."
Greg Keck

I first heard Greg Keck use that phrase in the mid-1990s to a room full of adoptive parents. There was a silent thud as our collective chins hit the floor. He explained that if you were being abused at least another human notices you; with neglect you may feel you don't exist. All present were deeply shocked. Many of us had been told by our social workers, "It's all right, they weren't abused, just neglected." I have used that phrase and expanded on the explanation to many groups; they too are shocked, yet all comprehend its significance. I hope the judiciary will soon.

Trauma overview
A child stores all his sensory experiences including the traumatic memories associated with abuse, neglect and chaos. Psychological trauma (referred to throughout the book as 'trauma') is generally defined by two conditions. An individual, adult or child, experiences either:

Δ overwhelming emotions which they are unable to integrate
    or
Δ a feeling they might die

If an individual can manage and integrate the feelings, resulting from a negative experience, it fails to be 'traumatic'. Obviously an adult can process these difficult feelings better than a child.

An infant uncontrollably screaming with rage, sobbing with fear, or frozen with anxiety has emotions that are overwhelming and traumatic. If there is no comfort, they feel they might die. Any prolonged episode of unresolved, overwhelming negative feelings constitutes childhood trauma and includes:
Δ Neglect
Δ Hunger
Δ Emotional & psychological abuse
Δ Physical abuse
Δ Persistent or unalleviated pain
Δ Chaos
Δ Sexual abuse
Δ Witnessing domestic violence – especially on the primary caregiver

BUBBLE WRAPPED CHILDREN

Repeated trauma distorts the physical, emotional, psychological and social development of that child. The issues arising for maltreated children compared to those of 'normal' children are considered in the next chapter.

One event: multiple perspectives and creation of sensory memories
The theory and written descriptions of maltreatment are one side of the story; however the sensory experience and the perceptions of each participant are another. Let's view "one event" from several perspectives and notice the sensory elements.

Imagine the scenario. A neighbour has reported another loud, violent fight and items are being thrown. Adults are shouting, screaming "I'll kill you", children are crying, dogs howling. This family has been being "known" to the police and Social Services for years. The children are on the 'at risk' register, and had odd periods in respite foster care. It is decided by police and social services that these children need to be "rescued" from their alcohol abusing parents immediately.

Through the baby's eyes

Baby Tim is in his cot, hearing the screaming, his mother sounding terrified, an enormous crash, his father raging again. He smells his own sweat and faeces, the stale urine, feels the thin yellow blanket, crinkled and crackly with stale milk. Tim bites his finger nails, the metallic taste of blood somehow reassuring and eases the hunger pangs. In the shadows through the bars, he sees the urine-soaked

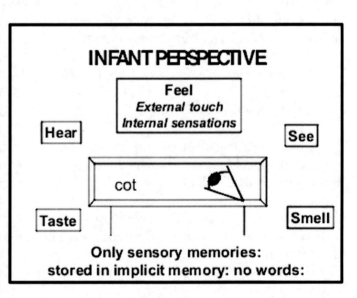

mattresses his sisters sleep on. The intermittent blue lights outside throw strange scary shadows on the wall. Tim hears the thumping of someone running up the stairs, light pours in as the door opens; a big man looks down at him, disgust on his face. Tim sniffs a strong scent, his heart races, while terror stiffens his entire body as the man's hands move towards him.

Through the policeman's eyes

The rugby-playing policeman fresh out of training has never seen such squalor. He has a nephew the age of this baby, but his nephew is not covered in sores, lying in own excrement. The room has three putrid mattresses, is bereft of toys or clothes with dog shit on the floor, yet at least four children sleep here. He gags picking up the soiled infant. With outstretched arms he carries the stinking baby downstairs into raucous chaos. The aggressive drunk parents are being arrested, the father pinned to the floor by his colleagues. The same colleagues who earlier had teased him about his over-enthusiastic use of Calvin Klein aftershave.

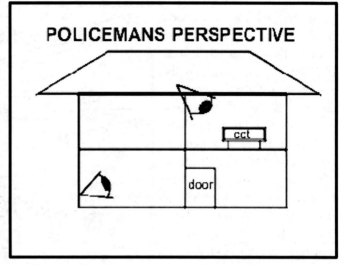

Through the social worker's eyes

As the duty social worker, Clare never quite knew what her shift would involve. Police breaking down a door and eventually bringing out four children under five after their parents had been taken away was more challenging than usual. The helicopter focusing its search light on the house was useful, but had also attracted spectators and the press. A local reporter was demanding to speak to her. Clare didn't know how to handle them or what she would do with four filthy hysterical infants at 2am on a cold, wet November night.

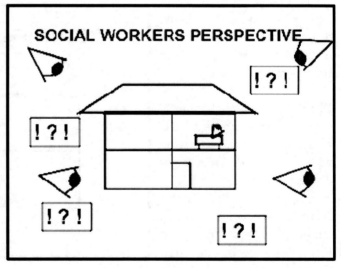

BUBBLE WRAPPED CHILDREN

Through the neighbour's eyes

Mr and Mrs Average were both relieved and concerned by the night's events. Living next to that family had been like walking on egg shells. When sober they were just about OK, but drunk there was no reasoning with them and no peace. The Averages felt so sorry for the children, which is why they called the police, but feared revenge from the drunks later. They often felt guilty about ignoring the children's cries – their grandchildren were the same age, but what else could they do? The helicopter and police seemed well coordinated; there were so many of them. The ambulance crew were treating a policewoman and one of the parents. It made the TV dramas seem quite tame.

Through the birth parents' eyes

Birth Father likes a drink and hates being disrespected. The kids irritate him and only the baby is his offspring.

Birth Mum likes having a strong man around the place, she enjoys partying with him and friends at home or in pubs or clubs.

Neither remember much about the event, except that this night was different because police and Social Services took the kids away, despite their attempts to stop them. Alcohol and the red mist of anger make the event almost impossible for either of them to recall.

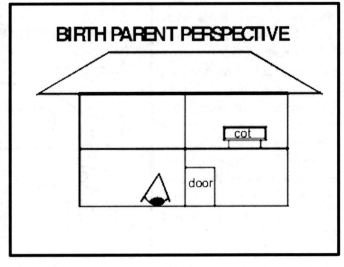

Each of the participants had a different perspective, experience and memory of this event. For the baby it was totally sensory. So many sensory triggers would be associated with that traumatic removal. The smell of Calvin Klein aftershave, blue flashing police lights, a look of disgust on the policeman's face (interpreted as I am bad). Biting fingers till they bleed gives comfort, stale urine is familiar.

"The senses are the ministers of the soul."
Leonardo da Vinci

In Tim's file or Child Placement Report, this episode would probably be recorded on a chronology as something like "emergency removal from home". A single line, maybe two; nothing which records the scale or emotional impact of the event. Yet we can see that emotional abuse, chaos, domestic violence, neglect, pain and hunger are incorporated into this one scenario.

Readers who think this is a gross exaggeration, you are partly right. Helicopters make the graphic more fun. However the rest is utterly realistic and repeated regularly throughout the UK and beyond.

So ten years later when Tim's behaviour is aggressive and his adoptive parents are trying to get some therapeutic input, this event is just one of many. Its impact on him is unknown by all. He has no conscious, explicit memory of it; yet the unconscious, implicit memory of it haunts him and helps drive his current angry behaviour.

Tim's needs for comfort, food, nurturing, safety and sleep were not met that night, or on many others.

BUBBLE WRAPPED CHILDREN

CHAPTER 2

CHILDREN'S NEEDS THROUGH TIME

Children's developmental needs change with time. They always need food, safety and nurturing, yet each will be fulfilled differently depending on the age of the child. Pizza is harmful for a baby, but a major part of a teenager's diet. You hold the hand of a toddler crossing the road yet that safety oriented behaviour with a fifteen-year-old would be tactless. An infant cries to show unhappiness, while an unhappy twelve-year-old might be slam doors, sulk or be grumpy when unhappy; both need nurturing, but in different ways. The infant may be hungry or have a soiled nappy; the twelve-year-old's unhappiness could stem from thousands of things, so gentle questioning, listening and sensitivity are the skills needed by attuned, nurturing parents. A good, sensitive parent notices the presenting behaviour and then delves deeper to ascertain the root cause of an issue and responds in way that is appropriate to the age of the child and the current circumstances.

Wall metaphor
The metaphor of building a wall to show how children's developmental needs are built on earlier ones was developed by Adoption UK within their Piece of Cake training for adoptive parents in 2000. The wall is a graphic representation of how children's needs develop.

During the first year of life the brain grows from 400 grams to about 1,000 grams and millions of neural network connections are made. Ideally the vast majority of the needs are provided by the parents and a solid foundation is laid for the future.

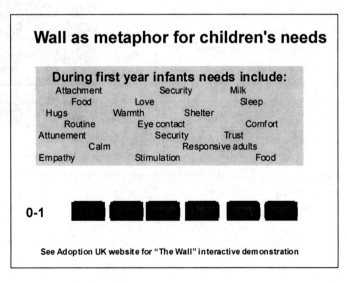

Wall as metaphor for children's needs

During first year infants needs include:

Attachment	Security	Milk
Food	Love	Sleep
Hugs	Warmth	Shelter
Routine	Eye contact	Comfort
Attunement	Security	Trust
Calm		Responsive adults
Empathy	Stimulation	Food

0-1

See Adoption UK website for "The Wall" interactive demonstration

In the following two years, many of the same needs remain and new ones are added.

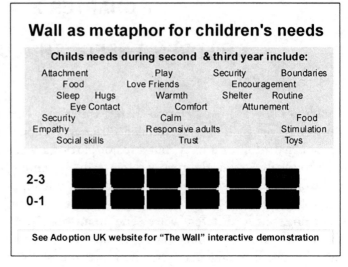

Ideally by adulthood, the metaphoric wall is solid, strong and robust. The individual has a solid sense of self or self-concept. Their inner working model, their map of the world and view of themselves is positive. They can function well in the world. Of course there will have been hiccups, small episodes of difficulty or some trauma, but the adults around them held them safe (literally and metaphorically) so they could learn and heal.

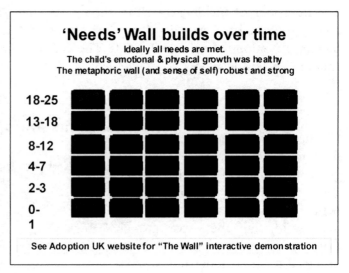

Sadly life is not like this for some children. Those with toxic parents have fragile unstable walls, because of the gaps, fractures and deficits, left by unmet needs. Maltreated children who experience trauma have walls with poor foundations, broken bricks and gaping holes. Their infancy needs were not met.

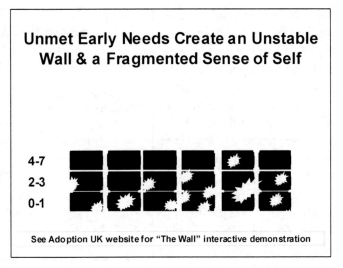

Unmet Early Needs Create an Unstable Wall & a Fragmented Sense of Self

4-7
2-3
0-1

See Adoption UK website for "The Wall" interactive demonstration

Also the child's experience in the womb is highly significant as its part of their foundation for the future. Exposure to drugs, alcohol, high stress levels and a poor maternal diet will have a negative impact on the developing foetus and bruise him before birth.

Even if the child subsequently has "good enough parenting" and future age appropriate needs are met, those earlier gaps will not be filled, hence as the child grows and the metaphoric wall is assembled, it becomes more and more unstable, because the base is poorly constructed and weak.

The only way to repair the infancy damage is with therapeutic reparenting throughout childhood and adolescence which in essence helps heal the trauma and fills in the developmental gaps. Infants and young children are bundles of emotion. They need an adult to help them control their overwhelming primitive emotions (fear, rage, disgust, separation anxiety) and become calm. They are incapable of regulating themselves. They learn self-regulation from a sensitive and empathetic parent responding appropriately to their emotion. This is part of the attachment process.

Attachment – an overview
Much has been written about attachment theory, which I will not repeat here. We know that the interactions between parents and infants determine the brain structure for children, which affects their mental processing including emotion and memory functions. Although the most significant time for learning attachment behaviour is during infancy, it may be partly corrected later with appropriate interventions. However the parent/baby stage is the most important because the infant's brain is growing and wiring so quickly.

BUBBLE WRAPPED CHILDREN

An infant or child who repeatedly has his emotional experiences safely contained and defused by a parent or caregiver will develop healthy attachment relationships and be likely to form positive views of themselves and their world. Ideally an infant will experience the repeated positive experiences illustrated below thousands and thousands of times.

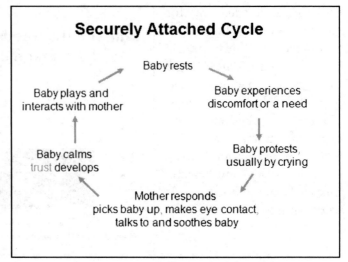

Securely Attached Cycle

Baby rests

Baby experiences discomfort or a need

Baby protests, usually by crying

Mother responds picks baby up, makes eye contact, talks to and soothes baby

Baby calms trust develops

Baby plays and interacts with mother

We make sense of our world through our sensory experiences. What we see, hear, taste, smell, feel and touch. From this data we make generalisations, we draw conclusions, we form assumptions, we build our own reality from this sensory input. This is our "map of reality" or "map of the world". Each person's unique representation of the world (map) is built from their individual perceptions and experiences. The first step in forming the map is our sensory experience.

Consider the experiences of an infant who is nurtured, loved, soothed and has his needs met. He experiences warmth, softness, harmony, laughter, cooing, smiling happy faces, hunger is soon satisfied, he cries and a familiar face responds to alleviate the mild distress.

He starts to generalise from these experiences. Remember, this infant has no words. He is starting to form an internal working model of himself and of the world via his senses. His internal representation of the world is being constructed, a map is being drawn. The diagram suggests some possible beliefs that a securely attached child may form.

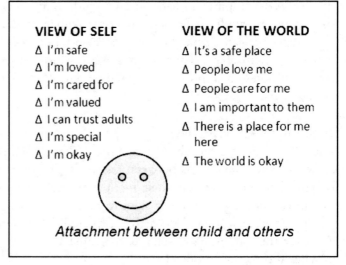

VIEW OF SELF
Δ I'm safe
Δ I'm loved
Δ I'm cared for
Δ I'm valued
Δ I can trust adults
Δ I'm special
Δ I'm okay

VIEW OF THE WORLD
Δ It's a safe place
Δ People love me
Δ People care for me
Δ I am important to them
Δ There is a place for me here
Δ The world is okay

Attachment between child and others

Fortunately most children get good enough parenting and form secure attachments. Readers should also understand that children are flexible and the occasional times when you don't "get it right" will not scar your child forever. The healthy pattern has been established, the child can make sense of their experiences, including the brief hiccups when a parent is not quite good enough. There has been sufficient consistent behaviour to establish a pattern which makes predicting future behaviour easier so trust can develop.

Trust as a concept is rarely broken down within the child care world. Although the Trust Model is covered fully in Chapter 10, it's worth examining three ingredients here because trust is such a key factor in infant attachment theory. The relevant trust components are:

   Δ Credibility – belief in someone's ability and competence due to their track record
   Δ Reliability – confident the person can be depended upon consistently
   Δ Intimacy – how comfortable and safe you feel with that person

From the child's perspective all three must be present for healthy attachment patterns to be formed. Credibility is related to past experiences, reliability focuses more on the future, while intimacy is totally in the present moment. For an infant all experiences are sensory and until at least eighteen months only stored in the implicit memory. So the development of trust can be derailed in many ways.

Brain development

It's worth a tiny digression into neuroscience here. We know there are different parts of the brain and neuroscience is demonstrating that the environment, adult behaviour, stimulation, diet, fear, attachment patterns will affect how the neural networks in an infant, child, adolescent and adult develop. Additionally the science of epigenetics illustrates how specific genes are switched on or off by internal processes, external stimuli and chemicals.

We know the brain is plastic. It can and will form new neural pathways and it will prune seldom used pathways. Neurons that fire together wire together. This happens most in early infancy then as toddler, young child, then a major pruning and rewiring process happens during adolescence.

   Δ At birth the infant brain weighs about 400 grams, by one year it's about 1,000 grams, by late adolescence it's at its maximum, about 1,400 grams. This increase is due to rapid generation of nerve cells (neurons) and supporting cells
   Δ Connections (axons and dendrites) being formed between neurons
   Δ Myelination. To ensure efficiency and speed of transmission the most frequently used connections are insulated with myelin, a fatty sheath.

BUBBLE WRAPPED CHILDREN

Maltreated children's brains will be wired differently from those of the securely attached child which will affect their present and future behaviour.

Disturbed Attachment Cycle

Consider a neglected child lying in a cot. He has an ache in his stomach from hunger; the thin dirty yellow blanket gives him no warmth. His nappy is heavy, stinking liquid trickles down his leg. He can taste sour milk, it's dark and he sometimes hears angry voices and crashing puncturing the silence. He smells his own stale sweat and the fragrance of dog dirt. He forms his "map of reality". He may metaphorically start wrapping himself in bubble wrap as a protection strategy.

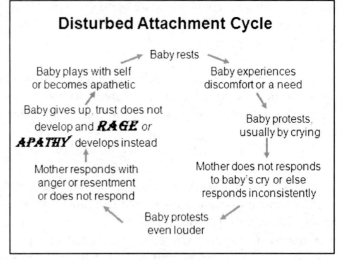

This infant has great swathes of time when the parent ignores their crying or reacts inappropriately. Some parents are inconsistent, on occasions responding appropriately, and at other times ignoring the child. Their parenting style may change because of drugs, alcohol or the presence of others. The children might also experience a succession of caregivers with very different methods and standards of child care. It is the lack of consistent care giving behaviour which is so distressing to the child. Without intimacy, credibility and reliability children can't make sense of the world.

VIEW OF SELF	VIEW OF THE WORLD
Δ I'm not safe	Δ It's a terrifying hostile world
Δ I'm not cared for	
Δ I'm scared	Δ People hurt you
Δ I'm unlovable	Δ Dangerous place
Δ I'm ignored	Δ No one could ever love me
Δ I'm not valued	Δ I am not important
Δ I'm alone	Δ There is no place for me
Δ I'm bad	Δ The world is dangerous
	Δ The world is not okay

Poor attachment between child and others

A world with no pattern or regularity makes predictions impossible. These apparently random, patternless, chaotic interactions are deeply disturbing for the child, disrupting their ability to trust and form healthy attachments to others.

Maltreated children have learned that adults can't be trusted and often hurt you. These beliefs stay with them whichever environment they inhabit.

A securely attached child will hold onto positive beliefs and an empowering view of the world, while maltreated children will grip their negative beliefs and view of a fear saturated world. As adults we don't change our beliefs when we move to a new country, city or new job. Why would we? Belief modification takes time and insight. The same is true for children, except they don't have the cognitive functioning for insight and reflection, hence are even less likely to change their deeply imbedded infancy beliefs. Remember the old Jesuit saying: "Give me a child until he is seven and he is mine for life."

There are several different classifications of 'attachment disorder' which depend on the particular experiences of the child, the parenting style and nature of the maltreatment. These feature in Chapter 3 as the product of different types of care giving. Obviously in addition to attachment behaviours there are many other factors influencing the developing child as the following diagram maps out.

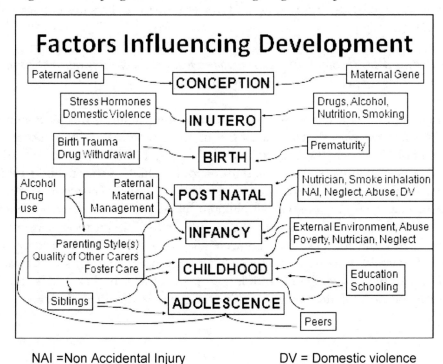

Factors Influencing Development

NAI =Non Accidental Injury   DV = Domestic violence

BUBBLE WRAPPED CHILDREN

Bruised before birth

One stage is worth a special mention: the foetal experience in the womb. Bathed with happy hormones, from a nutritionally conscious, happily expectant mother who laughs, rests and is relaxed, the foetus will grow healthily and contentedly. By contrast a mother who smokes weed or crack, has drinking binges, lives a chaotic stressed, anxious life with a violent man will bathe her (possibly unwanted) foetus in stress hormones. We know that alcohol and drugs affect the brain formation, particularly in the first trimester when women often don't know they are pregnant. Some adopted children, often undiagnosed, sit somewhere on the Foetal Alcohol, Spectrum Disorder, while others had drug withdrawal symptoms at birth and bear the physiological and psychological legacy. Both affect their thinking abilities. These children are bruised before birth, yet measuring this damage is almost impossible.

Care planning

The most critical time for a child is infancy and early childhood. That is why robust decisions about children should be made quickly and carefully based on sound evidence by skilled professionals who can be objective and hold the child at the absolute centre of the decision making process, not swayed by sympathy for the birth family or fear of them. Although the adults have legal rights and need consideration, the overarching focus and centre of attention must be the child. Unfortunately, sometimes the child's voice and perspective is lost in the cacophony of protests and distortions created by the birth family and the legal process. This has implications for care planning.

"Insanity is doing the same thing over and over again and expecting different results."
Albert Einstein

Too often children are left with toxic parents during infancy, the most important time of brain development. There are birth mothers who have kept a succession of children until they were twelve, eighteen or twenty-four months, then had each removed by Social Services. After the third or fourth child a pattern is noticeable, yet often action is not taken sufficiently early. There is much anecdotal evidence of women producing four/eight/twelve children all of whom are removed by Social Services, but often not until they hit the "terrible twos". Even though very little in their lives had changed, these mothers were allowed to try afresh each time, as if it was their first child. Each case is assessed in isolation, rather than seen as part of a pattern. Each time, fresh grief and loss for the birth mother and a traumatic experience for each of the children. This strategy serves neither the child nor the mother.

How is this relevant to social networking?

You may be wondering how this all relates to the impact of social networking on adoption. Traumatised children often have a limited ability to manage their emotions, so anger, hyper-arousal and hyper-vigilance are exhibited through various 'challenging behaviours'. Adopted children were maltreated, their ability to trust is limited and they often have very negative beliefs about themselves. They are vulnerable. The birth family were, unintentionally, responsible for the creation of many of those beliefs. The sudden arrival of these family members into an adolescent's life, even through the 'virtual world', is destabilising because it retriggers old unconscious patterns, fear and implicit sensory memories from infancy. For a few young people it has been more than disturbing, it's been genuinely 'traumatic'. They were utterly overwhelmed, unable to integrate their massive emotional response. This compromised their daily functioning; jobs were lost and relationships damaged while drugs and alcohol were used to ease the pain and confusion.

Maslow's Hierarchy of Needs

There is one other model worth mentioning which is relevant during an individual's entire life span, not just childhood. Developed in the 1950s, Abraham Maslow's Hierarchy of Needs explains how our needs motivate our behaviour and the lowest must be satisfied before we can address the higher needs as shown here in the original five stage model .

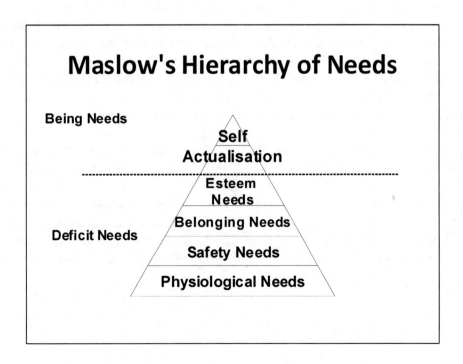

33

BUBBLE WRAPPED CHILDREN

We must have our 'deficit' needs met first and in this order.
- Δ Physiological needs include food, drink, shelter, warmth, sleep
- Δ Safety needs include protection, security, boundaries, order
- Δ Belonging needs include love, family, affection, relationships
- Δ Esteem needs include achievement, status, reputation, independence and responsibility

Only when we feel physically comfortable, safe, loved and recognised can we focus on realising our potential, aesthetics, self-fulfilment, beauty, knowledge and meaning.

However if any of our lower needs are not met, then self-actualisation needs just melt away. If you're in an art gallery with a full bladder, your appreciation of the pictures is blocked by the physiological messages telling you to 'go pee'. If a child is in a maths class, but fears he may be accosted on the way home, he is not motivated to learn Pythagoras theorem. A message the previous evening from a birth family member via Facebook would have the same destabilizing and distracting effect.

Maslow's Hierarchy of Needs is a useful model to have in the back of your head as a reference, because it can help make sense of what may appear to be strange behaviour. Children who have been abused will be particularly sensitive to anything that makes them feel unsafe and mostly the triggers will be unconscious. A child who was hit around the head will flinch if an adult gestures to ruffle their hair or pat their shoulder in praise. The girl for whom a hand on the knee in her birth family was the signal to go upstairs where she would be sexually violated, reacts hysterically when, after falling on the netball court, the PE teacher tends to her grazed knee. This trauma-triggered response appears 'out of proportion', to the minor injury, but the girl feels utterly unsafe and terrified, so for her unconscious mind, the reaction makes complete sense because screaming in the past may have prevented abuse.

In school some children may need to sit next to a wall or at the back of the class to feel safe. The neglected child who was frequently hungry may need to know the exact time for lunch and precisely what's on the menu. The child who lives in a chaotic home with no regular bedtime is unable to concentrate in lessons because he is too tired. Because his physiological needs have not been met, his academic progress is blocked. Some schools, recognising this, offer breakfast to pupils before school and noticed a measurable improvement in pupils' academic performance and behaviour.

Boundaries and teenagers

Children need boundaries to feel safe. The role of a good parent is to provide age-appropriate boundaries which keep the child safe, yet allow exploration, curiosity and challenge in their lives. This is as true at fourteen as four; however both the boundaries and the testing behaviour are different. Many adopted children hit the boundaries very hard during the teenage years and trying to keep them on track is a big challenge for parents and teachers. Sometimes keeping them 'safe' is impossible because of their risk taking behaviour, their flouting of rules, curfews and collaboration. I thought my kids were reasonable at sticking to curfews. Only years later did I discover that one came home on time, then climbed out through a window after I was asleep to continue 'partying' in an unknown location. I was in a ground floor flat, so it was quite easy to sneak in and out. A friend was alerted to her son's frequent absconding because creaking woke her at 2am when he climbed across the conservatory roof. Despite much discussion he ignored all the dangers associated with clambering over rain swept glass in the dark, because his overarching desire was to see friends.

How is this relevant to social networking?

Vulnerable teenagers will agree to meet someone online, not tell the responsible adults or friends and expose themselves to potential harm. There are adopted teenagers who have met up with members of their birth family without telling their adopters or anyone else. These liaisons have involved lengthy rail journeys to unknown places, online messaging, furtive texts and phone calls. The emotional energy required for such meetings will distract a teenager from all other activities for weeks or months. He will be tightly wound up like a spring, so therapeutic reparenting is impossible, studying difficult, normal life suspended as his behaviour will probably be dreadful; yet the adults around him don't know the root cause of this particular difficult phase.

Any reader thinking the adopters are at fault because the boy is not talking to them should remind themselves that the job description for a teenager includes being secretive and withdrawing from parents; more about that in Chapter 15. When teenagers eventually tell adopters about reconnecting with birth family members, much CRAP (Charged Reactive Angry Particles) has already been thrown around.

BUBBLE WRAPPED CHILDREN

CHAPTER THREE

PARENTING FROM OUTSTANDING TO TOXIC

"What lingers from the parent's individual past, unresolved or incomplete, often becomes part of her or his irrational parenting."
Virginia Satir

In my experience, birth parents whose children were removed by the courts carry great scars. Many of those scars existed before pregnancy; the intervention of the state which labelled them unfit parents wounded them further. Maybe a baby gave them something to love and be loved by: the dream that this child would fill the emotional gaps in their life. For others pregnancy was an unplanned event which might get them housing. A few desperately wanted a baby. The motives vary hugely, but like all other parents the original motivation are self-centred, to fulfil their own needs. However, unlike the vast majority of parents, these adults were not able to change the focus of their attention from themselves to the baby, infant or child. Their own needs remained the centre of their attention.

Frequent characteristics of parents who lose parental responsibility
These parents are rarely able to:
- Δ   see the world from the child's point of view
- Δ   see the harm their lifestyle is doing to the child
- Δ   see the harm their behaviour is doing to the child
- Δ   consistently parent at an adequate level
- Δ   change their behaviour
- Δ   fully engage with professionals such as social workers, lawyers and medics

These parents frequently:
- Δ   had a difficult or abusive childhood themselves
- Δ   have unresolved trauma from their own childhood
- Δ   are self-medicating with drugs and/or alcohol
- Δ   are unable to care for themselves adequately
- Δ   had no decent parenting roles models themselves
- Δ   see themselves as victims
- Δ   believe they own their child
- Δ   believe their child should stay with them whatever their lifestyle or circumstances
- Δ   have limited emotional intelligence and/or executive functioning i.e. thinking skills

BUBBLE WRAPPED CHILDREN

Reasons some birth parents are unable to properly care for their children:
- Δ Drug abuse
- Δ Alcohol abuse
- Δ Serious mental health issues
- Δ Major learning difficulties
- Δ Uncontrollable anger /violence

These parents always:
- Δ love their children

Even though the last characteristic may seem a strange one to include, given the behaviour of some birth parents, it is vital to acknowledge that these parents loved their children in the best way they could. Their definition of love, experience of love and ability to demonstrate loving behaviour may not be the same as yours or mine, but they loved and love their children. Yes; past and present tense. They never stop loving them, which starts to explain why birth parents will use social networking to find their loved ones. Wouldn't you?

"I love my children, so you can't take them away" is a sentiment often heard from birth parents during removal. Their demonstration of 'love' and 'loving behaviour' is not child-centred or what the child needs, but it's all that parent can offer. Their display of loving behaviour does not even reach the threshold criteria for inadequate parenting, their parenting is toxic. However, that parent does love that child.

Outstanding parenting
Love means different things to different people. In the film Love Actually, the character Karen, played by Emma Thompson, has the following conversation with her young daughter Daisy.

K.   So what's this big news then?
D   We've been given our parts in the nativity play.
K   Oooohhh (excitedly)
D   And I'm the lobster.
K   The lobster?
D   Yes.
K   In the nativity play?
D   Yes … First Lobster.
K   There was more than one lobster present at the birth of Jesus?
D   Dhheerrr!

This is a beautiful demonstration of outstanding parenting, because despite her own misgivings and thoughts, Karen mirrors her daughter's excitement, shares her joy and subsequently makes a brilliant costume. She attends the play, is effusive, yet genuine in her praise to Daisy, despite the emotional horrors which started exploding in her own life that day. Karen is able to put her children's needs above her own by smiling and being joyful on the surface, while wretched inside; an example of exceptional parenting.

Outstanding parents have their child's needs as their core focus while also caring for themselves too. Martyrdom is not necessary or desirable as it offers the wrong behavioural model to a child. Chapter 11 details excellent parenting traits.

Linking parenting style and children's behaviour

Even though the connection between parenting style and children's behaviour is a no-brainer, it's not always made by practitioners. Professor David Howe, from the University of East Anglia, explains that causal link, summarised on the next page in the two diagrams. Although brief, it gives some insight into how the three classifications of insecure attachments result from different parenting styles. Readers can compare and contrast the caregiver characteristics which are then reflected in specific children's behaviours.

Insecure Attachments
Caregiver Characteristics

Ambivalent	Avoidant	Disorganised
Δ Insensitive	Δ Rejecting	Δ Frightening
Δ Under involved	Δ Hostile	Δ Frightened
Δ Inconsistent	Δ Cold	Δ Helpless
Δ Anxious	Δ Conditional	Δ Abdication of responsibility
Δ Uncertain	Δ Intrusive	
	Δ Controlling	

Insecure Attachments
Typical Children's Behaviour

Ambivalent	Avoidant	Disorganised
Δ Hyper activation of attachment	Δ Defended	Δ Fear/compliance
Δ Coercive	Δ Emotions inhibited	Δ Compulsive caregiving
Δ Passive	Δ Compliant	Δ Rage + Fear + Sadness = controlling aggressive
Δ Dependent	Δ Self sufficient	
Δ Need + Anger	Δ Independent	
	Δ Anger + Fear	

Toxic parenting

Dr Forward, a renowned therapist and author, noticed a common emotional blind spot in thousands of her clients. Few made the connection between their upbringing and their current problems. In her book "Toxic parents - overcoming their hurtful legacy and reclaiming your life" Dr Forward says, *"A toxic parent has negative patterns of behaviour which are consistent and dominant in the child's life... The adult children of toxic parents suffer similar symptoms – damaged self-esteem, leading to self destructive behaviour... They almost all feel worthless, unlovable and inadequate."*

She categorizes six different subsets of toxic parents.
- Δ **The inadequate parents**: *"constantly focussing on their own problems, they turn their children into "mini-adults" who take care of them."*
- Δ **The controllers**: *"they use guilt, manipulation, and even over-helpfulness to direct their children's lives."*
- Δ **The alcoholics**: *"mired in a denial and chaotic mood swings, their addiction leaves little time or energy for the demands of parenthood".*
- Δ **The verbal abusers**: *"whether overtly abusive or subtly sarcastic, they demoralise their children with constant put downs and rob them of their self-confidence."*
- Δ **The physical abusers**: *"incapable of controlling their own deep-seated rage they often blame their children for their own ungovernable behaviour."*
- Δ **The sexual abusers**: *"whether flagrantly sexual or covertly seductive, they are the ultimate betrayers, destroying the very heart of childhood - its innocence."*

When the book was written in 1989, drug addiction was rarer and not included. Although the characteristics of alcohol and drug using parents are not identical many traits are similar.

No parent can be emotionally available all the time. Adequate parenting means protecting children from harm (physical and emotional); providing for their physical needs, providing love, attention and affection and giving moral and ethical guidelines. To parent adequately, nourishing, comforting, consistent behaviour is required. Without it children feel unloved.

Put simply – toxic parents are focused on themselves and their needs: adequate parents are focused on the child's needs.

Babies believe their parents are perfect. So do infants. So do toddlers. So do preschool children. If our parents are perfect we feel protected. *"Children soak up both verbal and non-verbal messages like sponges – indiscriminately... The things they learn at home about themselves and others become universal truths engraved deeply in their minds."* This imprinting occurs in the first seven years of life, during the next seven years we model – primarily our parents.

BUBBLE WRAPPED CHILDREN

With adequate parenting infants believe they are okay, they matter, they can trust the world and the people who care for them. Adequate parents understand that the two-year-old saying 'no' is asserting their independence. The three-year-old climbing on to the chair on his own is developing his unique identity and self will. Even though this behaviour may be inconvenient, an adequate parent sees it as a step on the journey towards healthy growth and independence.

"Toxic parents aren't so understanding. From toilet training through adolescence they tend to see rebellion or even individual differences as a personal attack. They defend themselves by reinforcing their child's dependence and helplessness." This has ramifications. Curiosity is seen as either 'naughty' or wilful disobedience to be criticised or punished, rather than recognised for its true role as a natural part of childhood innocence – to be encouraged and celebrated.

In my experience birthparents who have their children removed are toxic parents... who often had toxic parents themselves... who had toxic parents... who had toxic parents. Hence, without intervention, the cycle continues; generation after generation after generation after generation.

Although Susan Forward gives a chapter to each category of toxic parent, she recognises that there are many overlapping characteristics (denial, guilt, shame etc) resulting from different types of abuse. *"Incest victims often become very skilful child actors. In their inner world, there is so much terror, confusion, sadness, loneliness, and isolation that many develop a false self with which to relate to the outside world, to act as if things were fine and normal."* This false sense of self explains why some children when placed with an adoptive family may behave differently. It may also account for children who 'seem normal' despite known horrendous experiences.

"Abused children have the cauldron of rage bubbling inside them. You cannot be battered, humiliated, terrified, denigrated, and blamed for your own pain without getting angry. The battered child has no way to release this anger. In adulthood that anger has to find an outlet." Adopted children may show that anger to their adoptive parents and/or the world. Moving them from the original abusive environment opens up a chink through which the rage can vent. It does not remove or change the negative beliefs, fractured identity or pain. These will only change with significant therapeutic reparenting and input from therapists skilled in trauma work.

"It is abusive to launch frequent verbal attacks on the child's intelligence, appearance, competence, or value as a human being." Name calling and negative labelling often occur for 'at risk' children. Those wounds don't show, can't be placed on a court report, yet poison the child.

In the second half of her book, Dr. Forward offers processes and tools to help adults heal and also addresses the family system. She explains how the inner workings of a family system are barely visible on the surface. However their spoken and unspoken beliefs and rules dictate many basic assumptions about life.

"Toxic parents resist any external reality that challenges their beliefs. Rather than change they develop a distorted view of reality to support the beliefs they already have... As children of toxic parents grow up, they carry their parents' distorted beliefs unchallenged into their own adult lives."

If toxic parents resist any external reality, they don't change. They behave the way they always have. They believe what they always believed.

Toxic parents seldom accept the damage they have inflicted on their children.
- Δ "A good beating never did me any harm"
- Δ "He asked for it"
- Δ "She was safe in the cot all day, she stopped crying eventually"
- Δ "I'm a better mum after I've smoked a joint"
- Δ "I needed the booze and fags, not my fault I had no money left for food"
- Δ "She needs to know she's stupid"

When a child is adopted they bring this *'distorted view of reality'* into their new home. That view will not change just because the adopters are 'nice', feed them well and appear to consider their feelings. These kids 'know' it's just an act, because adults can pretend to be nice, sometimes for ages. They know adults are unpredictable and can't be trusted. In their eyes an adoptive parent is no different.

Sometimes adopted children impose their family system on their adoptive family. Siblings in particular, have a well established way of being. They operate as a team. The new adopters are the outsiders. The kids knew far more about family life and family systems than their adopters. Therapeutic reparenting offers a very different, nurturing, structured, systemic family model for the children and ideally will have been operating since placement. Contact via Facebook resurrects these old birth family systems for the child. This will contrast with the structure created by the adoptive parents, so conflict is created for the child which will probably be evidenced by their conduct and a fresh dose of 'challenging behaviour'.

Dr Forward is a proponent of short-term therapy and believes *"therapy is most effective when it proceeds down the double track: both changing current self-defeating behaviour and disconnecting from the traumas of the past."* RIGHT ON!

BUBBLE WRAPPED CHILDREN

CHAPTER FOUR

WHAT DO TOXIC PARENTS LACK?

Toxic parents exist all over the world, in every culture, every class, every profession and in both sexes. The children of some toxic parents live with them permanently, unidentified and unknown to the authorities. The children removed by the state and either fostered or adopted, failed to hurdle a very low bar. Why? What qualities, capabilities or skills do they lack? What is it they can't or won't do? In essence they lack insight, empathy and are focused wholly on themselves, but how are they *measurably* different from 'good enough' parents?

Some of the answers can, I think, be found in some psychological models and theories. Models are useful because they give a framework for thinking; it doesn't make them 'right'. They are simply tools which are visual, logical, relevant, measurable, share a common language and aid understanding. Hence there are diagrams and charts integrated throughout the book and particularly in this chapter.

Even though sociological and political factors are germane in proving solutions to the problems raised in adoption by social networking, no models are included because they shed little light on a specific individual's conduct and behaviour, which is my focus. However one point is worth noting. Although adopted and fostered children mainly come from the poorer and more deprived end of society, there are very many impoverished families who raise children with emotional warmth, healthy boundaries, encourage educational achievement and prioritise their children's needs and welfare. Equally there are affluent families who lack emotional warmth, while domestic violence spans all income groups. Even though having money makes parenting easier, its significance is lower than many other factors; in particular a person's ability to learn, change their behaviour and see things from another's perspective.

Nationally there are a variety of excellent parenting programmes, both formal and informal, funded by government or charities which help struggling parents and those who had poor parenting role models. These interventions are highly effective for individuals who have the capacity to learn from their mistakes and change their parenting style. My aim is to highlight the differences between parents who can and do benefit from these strategies and those who can't, by explaining some practical hows and theoretical whys.

Chaos

One of the common characteristics of families who have children removed by the state and subsequently adopted or fostered is their chaotic lifestyle and living environment. Good parents create a structured environment for children, (a framework not a rigid regime) and consistently provide a warm emotional atmosphere, meeting child's basic needs of safety, security and nurture. Chaotic families provide none of these.

Consistency is the key. It takes a certain level of thinking skills to plan, organise and cook regular meals, keep on top of the washing and cleaning, emptying rubbish, clear up spills while ensuring bills are paid. It's "housework". For many of us these dull repetitive tasks are rarely appreciated and don't get noticed until they are not done. Clearing up after children is never-ending, even if you've taught them to put their toys away, have organised and labelled their clothing drawers, have desk tidies and storage boxes. Children become excited, enthusiastic and forget because their thinking skills are less developed.

Organisational skills can be learned, evidenced by the many business and personal development management books published, demonstrating a common need and various solutions.

In my observation over two decades I have noticed certain patterns and characteristics of birth parents whose children were removed and subsequently adopted, particularly their lack of insight, ability to see things from the child's perspective, deficiencies in self-regulation and the ability to change their behaviour. The following models shed light in these areas, which are incidentally, also often a challenge for adopted children due to their earlier maltreatment. Some models overlap slightly, others stand alone. Their order is not significant.

Executive functioning skills

Executive skills are involved when we take and make decision. They help us decide which tasks or activities we will pay attention to and/or choose to do. They are high level cognitive functions generally undertaken within the prefrontal cortex, the most advanced part of the brain.

Executive skills allow us to organise our behaviour through time and override immediate demands or desires in favour of long-term goals. There are two components; thinking skills and behaviour regulators elaborated in the following charts adapted from Dawson and Guare's material.

	Thinking skills
Planning	Ability to create road map to reach goal or complete task. Ability to decide what is important and what to focus on
Organisation	Ability to arrange or place things according to a system
Time management	Allocation of time, recognition of deadlines, time frames and limits. Deciding on what is or is not urgent &/or important
Working memory	Ability to hold information in mind while performing complex tasks. Learn from past experiences. i.e. utilise past learning or bring old experiences to current situation. Future pace. Ability to project learnings and problem-solving strategies into the future.
Metacognition	See things from the outside. Ability to stand back and take bird's eye view of self in current situation. Ability to observe how you solve problems.

	Behaviour Regulators/ Emotional Skills
Response Inhibition	Ability to resist impulse to say or do something without thinking through the consequences. Capacity to think before you act.
Self regulation of Affect	Ability to manage emotions, control behaviour
Task Initiation	Ability to start task without undue procrastination
Flexibility	Ability to revise and change plans when obstacles, new information or mistakes occur. Adapt to changing conditions
Goal Directed Persistence	Capacity to follow through and complete task and not be diverted

Within "Executive Skills in Children and Adolescents," Dawson and Guare expand on each skill, offer ideas and coaching techniques to strengthen weaker skills. They also have questionnaires administered by therapists which parents and older children can complete and obtain detailed insights into individual strengths and weaknesses. My children certainly found it helpful.

Emotional intelligence
Emotional intelligence refers to the ability to perceive, control, and evaluate emotions. It embraces two aspects of intelligence.

Δ   Understanding yourself, your goals, intentions, responses and behaviour
Δ   Understanding others and their feelings.

BUBBLE WRAPPED CHILDREN

Daniel Goleman author of "Working with Emotional Intelligence" presents five core competencies or domains.

	Emotional Intelligence Core Domains
Self awareness	Knowing your emotions Awareness of own feelings and ability to use them as a guide to better decision making. Knowing one's own abilities and shortcomings.
Self regulation	Managing your own emotions Able to recover from emotional distress, manage our emotions, being conscientious and delay gratification
Motivation	Motivating yourself Develop achievement and goal orientation, so frustrations and setbacks are put in perspective
Empathy	Recognising and understanding other people's emotions Awareness of what others are probably thinking or feeling
Social skills	Managing relationships – managing the emotions of others Interacting well with people in both close personal relationships and wider social networks

Emotional intelligence is

Δ   Recognising our own feelings and emotions and learning how to express them in an appropriate way at appropriate times

Δ   Being able to empathise with others and work with them

Δ   'Learnable' and 'Improvable'. We can all choose to improve our emotional intelligence

Each of the five domains can be expanded. Within the context of how Facebook impacts present and future adoption practice, the first two competencies are particularly relevant and worth more consideration because of their link to birth parents functionality before and during the removal of a child and then decades later when reconnection via Facebook occurs. The next page has a list of competencies associated with self-awareness and self-regulation, taken from the Consortium for Research on Emotional Intelligence in Organizations EI Framework (www.eiconsortium.org) which has a full and extensive list for all five domains and more useful data.

Self Awareness EI Competences	People with this competence
Emotional awareness: Recognizing one's emotions and their effects.	Know which emotions they are feeling and why See the links between their feelings and what they think, do, and say Recognise how their feelings affect their performance Have a guiding awareness of their values and goals
Accurate self-assessment: Knowing one's strengths and limits	Aware of their strengths and weaknesses Reflective, learning from experience Open to candid feedback, new perspectives, continuous learning, and self development Able to show a sense of humour and perspective about themselves
Self-confidence: Sureness about one's self-worth and capabilities.	Present themselves with self-assurance; have presence. Can voice views that are unpopular and go out on a limb for what is right Are decisive, able to make sound decisions despite uncertainties and pressures

Self Regulation EI Competences	People with this competence
Self-control: Managing disruptive emotions and impulses	Manage their impulsive feelings and distressing emotions well Stay composed, positive, and unflappable even in trying moments Think clearly and stay focused under pressure
Trustworthiness: Maintaining standards of honesty and integrity	Act ethically and are above reproach Build trust through their reliability and authenticity Admit their own mistakes and confront unethical actions in others Take tough, principled stands even if they are unpopular
Conscientiousness: Taking responsibility for personal performance	Meet commitments and keep promises Hold themselves accountable for meeting their objectives Are organized and careful in their work
Adaptability: Flexibility in handling change	Smoothly handle multiple demands, shifting priorities, and rapid change Adapt their responses and tactics to fit fluid circumstances Are flexible in how they see events
Innovativeness: Being comfortable with and open to novel ideas and new information.	Seek out fresh ideas from a wide variety of sources Entertain original solutions to problems Generate new ideas Take fresh perspectives and risks in their thinking

BUBBLE WRAPPED CHILDREN

When making assessments about the capacity of a birth mother or birth father to care for a child long term, professionals could use emotional intelligence competencies as a method of monitoring a parent's behaviour. It identifies specific criteria which can be recorded, tracked and subsequently used in decision making. This reduces subjectivity and clarifies thinking. The information can be shared with birth parents to help them see where they may need to make more effort to prove their capacity to change or learn. A birth parent lacking emotional awareness and self-control, who screams, shouts abuse and has 'anger issues' could be very frightening for a child. Readers may notice how these characteristics map across to the characteristics of insecure attachments discussed in the previous chapter.

Reasonable emotional intelligence and executive skills allow us to:
- Δ   Be able to live in the present; plan for the future and contemplate the past
- Δ   Organise and manage our clothes, food, home, thoughts, shopping, money
- Δ   Be responsible: take responsibility for ourselves, acknowledge and learn from our mistakes
- Δ   Have cause and effect thinking: see the consequences of our behaviour, past and present
- Δ   Bite our lip and listen when we disagree, then calmly put forward our own opinion
- Δ   Hold our temper or anger, not lash out
- Δ   Have mindsight and empathy, be able to see and understand another's viewpoint and needs
- Δ   Defer pleasure activities when work or chores need to be done
- Δ   See potential dangers ahead and keep ourselves and others safe
- Δ   Recognise 'dodgy' or inappropriate behaviour from others

It could be said that a lack of emotional intelligence and executive functioning skills resembles immaturity. Quite so; the brain has not been able to wire itself in a way that allowed proper maturation. Hence those with reduced emotional intelligence and executive functioning may function at a much younger level than their chronological age would suggest. These are frequent features of birth parents whose children are removed by Social Services and the courts. Their children often display similar deficits too.

Another consequence is the behaviour inconsistency. These individuals can hold it together for a while, but not for long and not repeatedly; especially when stressed, anxious and during tough times. Hence a parent may demonstrate these competencies for a short while, maybe during regular contact sessions, but 24/7 is a very different matter; yet social workers and courts make decisions to reunite a child and birth mother based on this scant evidence.

CHAPTER FIVE

EMPATHY

"Never criticize a man until you've walked a mile in his moccasins."
Native American Wisdom

This quote assumes you can step into someone else's skin, look through their eyes, feel their joy and pain, and recognise their values, beliefs and motivations. That's a tall order. However, it's what outstanding parents do.

Although my focus in this chapter is empathy, it's worth quickly touching a very similar concept: mindsight. Daniel Seigel considers mindsight to be "the ability to perceive our own minds and the minds of others". It is one of his five parenting cornerstones, explored further within Chapter 11 on therapeutic reparenting.

Mindsight
Mindsight presupposes the ability to be fully inside ourselves and also the ability to step outside into another's standpoint. Within NLP these perspectives are termed First and Second Positions. In First Position it's your own reality; in Second Position it's the other person's world including their beliefs, values and their point of view; while the Third Position is the place to take an outside detached, dissociated view.

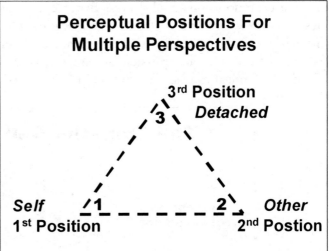

To act wisely and to benefit from hindsight you need all three perspectives. In Chapter 13, one event, multiple perspectives and different perceptual positions are illustrated as part of the healing process for a child. Exploring the different (perceptual) positions of birth parents, adopters, social workers and the individual child is a core principle flowing throughout this book.

Empathy

Simon Baron Cohen, a Cambridge University professor and expert in autism and developmental psychopathology, published "Zero degrees of Empathy" in May 2011. It's a terrific read and quotes here are in italics. He includes a questionnaire so you can discover your own EQ, and there are several 'how to spot' sections, including a young person with Conduct Disorder, a Narcissist, Psychopath and Borderline Personality Disorder. Three of his new ideas are particularly pertinent here: the empathy spectrum, the brain's 'empathy circuit' and his conclusions that empathy is the result of experiencing parental love and, although he does not use the term 'epigenetics,' the possibility of some genetic component.

Baron Cohen says *"empathy is our ability to identify what someone else is thinking or feeling, and to respond to their thoughts and feelings with an appropriate emotion"*. Thus there are two stages to empathy: firstly recognition then response.

Empathy can also fluctuate and be situational. Sometimes we may be preoccupied and self-focused and just not notice others. This may be momentary, temporary or for a larger chunk of time and affected by circumstances. If you are late for an appointment you may notice a work colleague in mild distress, but decide not to help because you have a higher priority. It you are also thinking about a sick friend you may not even notice his mild distress because you are so self-focused. Baron Cohen says *"empathy is more like a dimmer control than an all-or-none switch"*. He also suggests through measuring empathy and "there are such instruments, so this is not idle science fiction" that it's possible to assign everyone an 'empathy score', which follows the familiar normal distribution or bell-shaped curve.

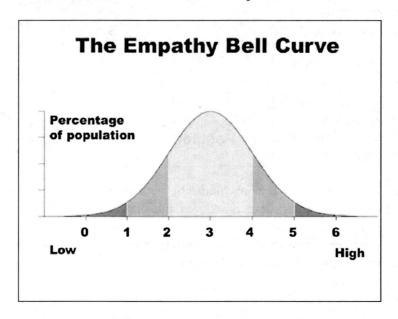

The Empathy Bell Curve

Percentage of population

0   1   2   3   4   5   6

Low   High

He has defined seven broad bands for his Empathizing Mechanism, or Empathy Spectrum, which are briefly summarised below and include the following membership characteristics:

- △ **Level Zero**: *"an individual has no empathy at all"*
    - ▲ For some they are capable of committing serious crimes
    - ▲ Some find relationships difficult but have no wish to hurt others
    - ▲ For others hurting another person *'means nothing to them'*, because they simply do not understand what another is feeling.
    - ▲ Level Zero includes Psychopaths, Narcissists and 'Borderline Personality types'.
- △ **Level One**: the person may be capable of hurting others, but can to some extent reflect on what they have done and show regret.
    - ▲ *"Empathy does not have sufficient brake on their behaviour"*
    - ▲ Someone 'sees red', with uncontrolled violence
- △ **Level Two**: a person still has difficulties with empathy but has enough insight to stop physical aggression, but they may shout or say hurtful things. They may need lots of feedback about the impact of their behaviour as they are often mystified as to what they are doing wrong.
- △ **Level Three**: a person knows they have difficulty with empathy and may adapt their lives accordingly.
- △ **Level Four**: "a person has a 'low-average' amount of empathy", friendships may be based more on activities than emotional intimacy and offering practical solutions
- △ **Level Five**: higher than average empathy, an individual has good mindsight, compassion and an awareness of others' feelings
- △ **Level Six**: remarkable empathy; constantly focused on others' feelings and go out of their way to be supportive. *"It's as if their empathy circuit is in a constant state of hyper-arousal."*

Baron Cohen says that though our empathy may fluctuate, *"the band we are in is broadly fixed"* and it is this aspect which is particularly relevant to the impact of social networking on adoption. If a birth parent was in Level Zero or Level One when their child was removed, then five, ten, fifteen or twenty years later they may still have little insight into the impact of their behaviour on the child in the past, present or future.

He says the setting of the empathy mechanism *"depends on the functioning of a special circuit of the brain, the empathy circuit"* which consists of at least ten specific interconnecting brain regions. Although this book does not delve deeply into how trauma affects infant, child and adult brain development and functioning;

identification of an empathy circuit provides us with a huge piece of the jigsaw to start understanding the 'why', 'what' and 'how' of childhood trauma. Also remember that the vast majority of birth mothers, whose children were removed and adopted, experienced ghastly childhoods themselves so the poor empathy circuit passes from generation to generation through toxic parenting, not genetic inheritance.

Zero degrees of empathy

Baron Cohen explains that *"Zero degrees of empathy means you have no awareness of how you come across to others, how to interact with others or how to anticipate their feelings or reactions"*. Fundamental parenting skills, I would argue. *"It creates deep-seated self-centeredness, other people's thoughts and feelings are just off your radar."* By contrast good parents consciously tune into their child's needs and emotional state. *"For those who come into the orbit of someone with depleted empathy it means the risk of being on the receiving end of verbal insults, physical attacks... in short, at risk of getting hurt."* Baron Cohen describes three specific categories of DSM-IV (Diagnostic and Statistical Manual of Mental Disorders), psychiatric or 'personality' disorders which sit under his umbrella of Zero degrees of empathy; Borderline Personality Disorder (referred to as Borderlines), Psychopath and Narcissist.

Mentalising the caregiver's mind

Peter Fonagy, quoted by Baron Cohen, contends that *"during the attachment relationship, the infant tries to 'mentalise' the caregiver's mind... he argues that developing empathy proceeds well only if it is safe to imagine another person's thoughts and feelings".*

"Only"!!

"Only, if it is safe to imagine another person's thoughts and feelings." Pause for a moment, reflect on the attachment cycle in Chapter 2 and then ask yourself, "Is it safe for an infant to 'mentalize' the mind of an abusive, neglectful parent?" What pictures does that maltreated infant form? How can this child develop empathy?

Just imagine what life is like for John who is parented by a mother with Borderline Personality Disorder. She shouts and swears at him when he doesn't do what she wants. She might walk out leaving him alone, slam doors, threaten to kill herself, then within minutes be laughing and joking, then another behavioural switch occurs and she confronts neighbours aggressively. Soon afterwards she is weeping, then screaming, oblivious to the impact on her son or anyone else.

Poor John. The parent who should protect him and be his safe base is also the source of his terror. This is the classic combination for the development of disorganised attachment disorder.

Imagine Suki's life with her psychopath father. His surface charm is enticing and can generate a succession of friends or lovers continuously moving through his life. A beguiling, superficially attractive man, but the contrasting cruelty, his lies and dishonesty pop up frequently. Does that smile on his face mean something nice is going to happen, or is the precursor to an act of premeditated cruelty? Suki can't tell, but she does learn that a smile on any adult's face could mean pain is imminent.

What happens if John and Suki are adopted? Fast forward a decade and these two birth parents with zero degrees of empathy could well be tracing and emailing John and Suki via Facebook. They want to reconnect because of their own needs and desires. The impact on John or Suki is simply not considered. For a zero empathy birth parent, the child's situation is irrelevant.

The distinction between 'traits' and 'states' is one further aspect of empathy relevant to adoption issues and worth highlighting, because it addresses the *'can this birth parent change?'* question. 'Traits' are permanent, solid configurations of the neural or psychological system which endure in different situations and are irreversible. By contrast, 'states' are fluctuations in the neural or psychological system, context related and reversible. External factors such as alcohol, drugs, grief or tiredness can temporarily affect our state.

The big question when making decisions about removing children from birth families is *'can these parents change sufficiently, within the time scale of the child?'* Is the current level of toxic parenting the result of a temporary issue, which with assistance might be transformed to good enough parenting, or is their zero empathy an unbending, fixed trait?

BUBBLE WRAPPED CHILDREN

CHAPTER SIX

LEARNING AND CHANGING

"I can't teach anybody anything; I can only make them think."
Socrates

The million dollar question in the child protection, adoption and fostering world is, "does this birth parent have the capacity to change, and if so by when?" Can they alter their mindset and learn the necessary skills? What evidence would demonstrate a mindset shift? What behavioural changes would indicate learning has occurred?

This chapter highlights some possible blocks to an individual's learning and examines the learning cycle. These models are used in the corporate world and I believe are useful here because they offer more tools to understanding an individual's underlying processing strategies and specific ways they could be enhanced.

The more you know, the more you know you don't know

Bizarre as it may seem, one of my aims in writing this book is to increase the amount that you the reader recognise that you don't know. As your knowledge and experience increase, so the boundary between the known and the unknown expands, as illustrated in the diagram. The boundary line that sits between known and unknown gets longer and longer. This increases uncertainty. The point being simply, 'the more you learn, the less you know and understand.'

BUBBLE WRAPPED CHILDREN

For some people uncertainty is difficult; they prefer life to be black and white, good or bad rather than black, white and multiple shades of grey. Grey means doubt and the possibility of changing views and beliefs once held to be absolute truths. Grey means admitting you were wrong, accepting new ideas, absorbing fresh perspectives. This takes courage.

> *"Courage is not the absence of fear but rather the judgement that something else is more important than fear."*
> Ambrose Redmoon

Learning new material or new skills or new behaviour or new emotions takes courage because you are moving outside your comfort zone into unknown territory which does not feel safe. You often have to overcome fear. Sometime the fear is tiny and easy to confront, other times its much harder. Your character and life experiences will determine how much risk you are prepared to take in learning new things.

Sometimes you may be working with an individual and whatever you tell them, teach them or show them, they simply don't seem to get it. Their behaviour does not change, or just modifies temporarily. Chaotic families often display this characteristic. Learning theories may offer professionals a framework to step back and assess the current situation more clearly and have more evidence to predict future scenarios.

Learning cycle
We learn throughout our life. We are the product of what we have learned. Our experience in infancy, childhood, adolescence and in our adult life shapes who we are, how we think and what we do.

Our ability to process information, analyse and modify our behaviour using our prefrontal cortex is one of the things that separate us from animals. Humans have the ability to reflect, step back and consider other options, put ourselves in another's shoes, plan months or years ahead, be insightful. We can use the tools of mindsight and perceptual positions discussed in the previous chapter.

Learning is the gateway to every other capability we might want to develop. We acquire new skills and new knowledge using the learning process; whether it's driving a tank, scuba diving, creating a website, acquiring a new language, public speaking or having fabulous relationships.

Discovering more about how we learn makes us better learners and better educators.

David Kolb is generally credited with launching learning styles theory in the early 1970s. He suggests *"learning is the process whereby knowledge is created through the transformation of experience. Knowledge results from the combination of grasping experience and transforming it".* This cycle begins in quadrant 1 'why' in the diagram below and progresses clockwise forming a natural cycle of learning.

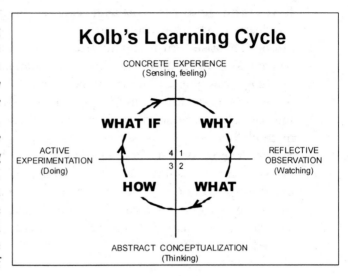

In 1982 Honey and Mumford published their Manual of Learning Styles accompanied by a questionnaire which helped people work out their preferred learning style. Their terms are slightly different; their stages are experiencing, reviewing, concluding and planning. To truly 'learn', you must pass through each stage. Skipping a stage is a major block to learning because you don't complete the process.

Each of us has a quadrant where we prefer to start our learning and possibly a quadrant that we (unconsciously) avoid. By identifying your preferred learning style you can discover your preferences and optimise your learning effectiveness. By strengthening an under-utilised learning style preference you can significantly increase your capacity to learn easily and effortlessly. You can discover your own learning style preferences by completing the learning style questionnaire available through Peter Honey

Different learning activities tend to be more compatible with certain learning styles.
- Δ Strong Activists learn best from trying new and diverse experiences, generating ideas, crises, dramas, being thrown in at the deep end and just 'having a go'. They find it more difficult to learn from solitary work, repetitive practices, precise instructions, attention to detail, listening to lectures.
- Δ Strong Reflectors learn best from observing first, researching, having time and space to think. They find it more difficult to learn from activities that

force them into the limelight, expect spontaneous ideas or to reach conclusions with insufficient data.

Δ Strong Theorists learn best in structured situations with a clear purpose, when links between different ideas or situations are mapped out, being asked or asking searching questions and navigating complex situations. They find it more difficult to learn without purpose or guidelines, when emotions and feelings are emphasised, with messy unstructured processes and dodgy methodology.

Δ Strong Pragmatists learn best when there is an obvious link between a current problem and the subject matter, by watching a demonstration, seeing the practical application and ideally being able to implement it immediately. They like the 'how to' tips. They find it more difficult to learn from 'chalk and talk' lecturing, pure unapplied research or activities which won't improve their immediate performance.

So what? How is this relevant to parenting traumatised children, contact with or without Facebook, care planning, government strategy, safeguarding services, court procedures, therapy, adoption support and all kinds of professional and personal decision making?

Simply that decisions need to be robust; well thought through, stand up to scrutiny, stand the test of time, be strong from all perspectives, have all possible avenues and options explored, be consistent and well constructed. This is best achieved by learning from past mistakes and projecting these learnings into the future.

As individuals, teams, organisations, government and legislative bodies we sometimes miss stages in the learning process. In "The Learning Styles Questionnaire", Peter Honey identifies four ways of distorting the learning cycle.

Remember all four stages of the learning cycle are crucial to the whole learning process. Skipping or ignoring one or more stages will impede or even prevent learning. The stages – experiencing, reviewing, concluding and planning – are mutually supportive and interdependent. Although you can start at any stage, and some might take longer than others, it is vital to follow the cycle, probably many times to really solidify all facets of the learning.

> *"Insanity is doing the same thing over and over again*
> *and expecting different results."*
> Albert Einstein

Distortion 1

In this distortion an individual, or organisation, becomes addicted to activities, being constantly on the go and 'doing things'. This results in rushing around and assuming that having an experience is synonymous with learning from them.

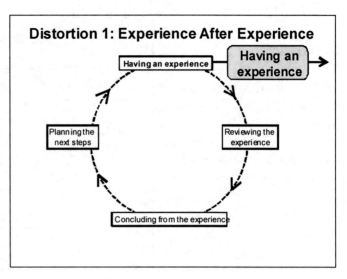

Distortion 2

People who postpone reaching conclusions or taking action because they want more information avoid 'doing' while pondering, resulting in 'analysis paralysis'. This could be seen as part of the problem within child care proceedings in the court system. Sometimes yet more 'expert reports' are requested which can delay the process and decision making by months, while the child remains stuck in the system.

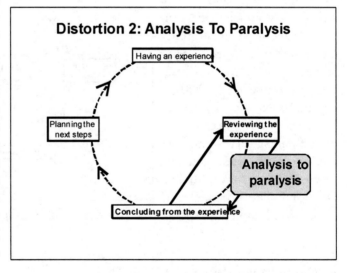

Distortion 3

Here the tendency is to quickly decide on a course of action without adequate analysis.

A quick fix is a tempting prospect for overworked social workers and other professionals with large case loads and poor supervision.

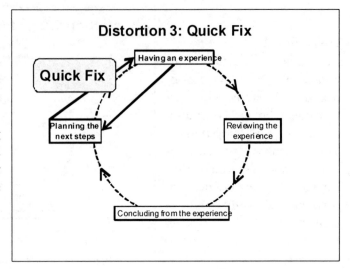

Distortion 4

People who want to reach an answer quickly can bypass the reflection and reviewing stage and jump straight to conclusions. In the review stage uncertainty and ambiguity are high, which can be uncomfortable. Within organisations such as Social Services or government departments there can be great pressure to achieve results and make quick decisions. The potential for

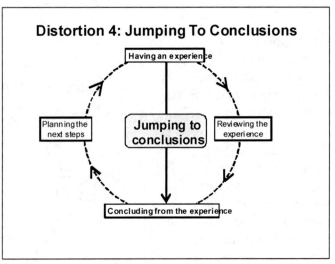

conclusion jumping, particularly under the media spotlight, could be overwhelming.

Learning from serious case reviews

"Serious case reviews are undertaken when a child dies (including death by suspected suicide), and abuse or neglect is known or suspected to be a factor in the death. Additionally, Local Safeguarding Children's Boards may decide to conduct an SCR whenever a child has been seriously harmed... and the case gives rise to concerns about the way in which local professionals and services worked together to safeguard and promote the welfare of children." Department of Health website.

Although serious case reviews are intended to learn lessons and improve services and should provide valuable lessons for child safeguarding practices, the learning seldom drifts to every corner.

Pat Beesley considers some of the main themes emerging from serious case reviews in "Identifying Neglect".

△ **Loss of focus on the child, focus on the adult.** *"Neglect cases are complex and difficult to work with... In some cases attention has been diverted, because of the disorganised and chaotic lives of the family, from the child to the adult. Practitioners have been "hijacked" by the adults."*

△ **Lack of overview or reflection on events.** *"Where this overview has missing, referrals or incidents have been seen in isolation and the true picture has not emerged until a serious incident occurs and a full chronology is undertaken... Several referrals may have been made to children's social care services and been dealt with as one-off referrals by duty teams, or may have been cases that were opened and closed a number of times with different practitioners involved."* This could be an example of the "quick fix" or "jumping to conclusions" distortion.

△ **Poor assessment and analysis.** *"Incomplete or poor assessments lacking in risk assessment and analysis are mentioned in many of the serious case reviews reports. Initial optimism about parenting capacity can become the dominant view, even in the light of later conflicting evidence... Leading to a 'rule of optimism' (Laming 2003) which then distorts the real picture."*

Sadly, Beesley also says *"It is however dispiriting to see that the themes and lessons of these reports are one that have been repeated since the first major review was undertaken, following the death of Maria Colwell"*. This suggests that learnings have not filtered through to practitioners at all levels within professional teams, departments and those who manage and oversee them. The 'rule of optimism', a phrase eloquently coined by Lord Laming, still governs many Social Services departments.

BUBBLE WRAPPED CHILDREN

CHAPTER SEVEN

SCREAMING: THE BIRTH PARENT PERSPECTIVE DURING THE REMOVAL PROCESS

The rule of optimism doesn't just exist for Social Workers; it is ever-present for birth parents too. They can't envisage their children being removed. Their children are "theirs"; reflecting the unspoken principle that parents "own" their own children. Yes, I know that sentence repeats 'their' and 'own', but the language we use talking about "our" children implies ownership and possession, so is worth flagging up. Hence to take from a parent their most valued possession, a child, is by any measure, huge; and that's what adoption does. No wonder the birth mother screams; loudly outwardly and/or silently inside.

In 1998 the charity After Adoption published "Still Screaming: Birth parents compulsorily separated from their children". It offers a unique perspective; mothers sharing their experience and crippling grief after the state intervened and removed their children. The quotes in this chapter are from contributors in the book. One reason I have used "Still Screaming" as a source is because these parents fit exactly into the demographic of those currently reconnecting with their adopted children on Facebook right now.

Within this chapter I am specifically referring to birth mothers, because although a few birth fathers are closely involved in day-to-day care for their children, the vast majority of children we are considering are raised by one mother. She may have a succession of partners, but the 24/7/365 responsibility is with her.

Again I use specific language. "24/7/365" is very different to a couple of hours every day or week, which is what occurs during 'contact' sessions when a child is in foster care and it is worth reminding ourselves of that distinction. We can all be on our "best behaviour" for a few hours; however our true self is only exposed when we live with someone 24/7/365. Just think of how many people you would not want to live with 24/7/365? I bet your list is quite long. Children live with a birth mum 24/7/365: they have no choice.

Before removal
Unless there is a single dramatic or horrific event which requires the immediate removal of a child from home, many birth mothers come to the notice of Social Services because they are struggling to cope. This could be identified before, during

or after the child is born. Many parents struggle to cope, but with support they can become "good enough" parents, however this takes time. Social workers visit a family, make assessments, provide resources (material or educative), offer advice and a helping hand. To do this the social worker needs to form a good relationship with the mother so trust can develop.

The social worker should be specific in what evidence and behavioural changes the birth mother needs to make. Social workers should also be very clear about unacceptable behaviour and the consequences of the birth mother not complying with these criteria. There is, metaphorically, a "game" being played with rules, timeframes, penalties and a playing field with boundaries. The term "game" was probably first used by Eric Berne in "Games People Play" where using Transactional Analysis principles he describes typical human relationships and interaction strategies which satisfy some inner motivation and have a payoff for the players but are often played to avoid real intimacy.

This is quite confusing for the birth mother. Does she fully understand the rules of the game? Also that 'friendly' social worker who is offering help is also the person who could recommend the child's removal. How much can, or should, the birth mother trust this person?

Many birth mothers express anger at the person they trusted, social worker or family helper, subsequently 'betraying them'.
"I thought she was my friend."
"We thought they were trying to help when all the time they were just watching for anything we did wrong."
What role did the social worker have? Friend or police officer?

Even though the birth mother is doing her best, it's way below acceptable standards. Often she can't comprehend how her behaviour is damaging her child. Her own emotional intelligence or executive functioning may be poor. She may feel unable to leave an abusive relationship. Her drug or alcohol consumption renders her incapable of decent child care. The bottom line is that her child is suffering greatly, needs to be removed and placed in a safe and nurturing environment.

Maybe she can't see or even remember what she did, or failed to do; hence can't acknowledge the hurt caused to her child. This has big implications for contact in later years.

At this stage a birth mother becomes increasingly disempowered and the grief process starts. She is losing her child. Again that language is far too mild, not 'losing'.

Her child is being forcibly ripped from her; 'stolen' by Social Services; 'taken away', 'put into care' and her legal parental rights will be terminated.

She is catapulted into bereavement and loss. She starts her grieving, a process she may never exit. Emotionally a birth mother will be shocked and disturbed. She may appear angry and uncooperative, maybe dissociated, maybe in denial, frozen, maybe depressed.

During the removal and court process: the game, players and rules change
"It became clear from all the birth parents who contacted us that court proceedings had a huge impact on their self-worth and self-esteem. Many felt betrayed by social workers who had been perceived as helpers and suddenly became opponents in the legal battle. This shift from one of enabler and partner to adversary was the most difficult for birth parents to take in and contributed to their anger towards the social worker." Still Screaming P39

Once Social Services decide that the child can't return to the birth mother, it's the start of a new 'game'. The playing field is a different shape, the rules have changed, and there are some new players. Contact arrangements are altered. Other social workers might be involved, the court process starts. There may be assessments by psychologists, various 'expert' reports written. The legal and social services processes though different intertwine and have many stages. The legal process is adversarial, the language academic, postponements and delays occur. It's a highly complex process.

For a poorly educated birth mother in the middle of an emotional crisis, it must be unfathomable and agonising.

Reports will document much of the birth mother's life, including many ugly aspects and private family affairs. Seeing that written down is disturbing and hurtful. How would you feel if all the bad events in your life were used as evidence against you? Just seeing them written down would shake most people's self-worth. We all have parts of our lives about which we feel guilty or ashamed. For the birth mother losing parental responsibility, it is written down, shared with many players and possibly voiced publicly in court proceedings. How deep does that shame go?

For many birth mothers who lose their children to adoption, their earlier life was difficult, chaotic, challenging and painful. Being publicly labelled an unfit mother is another huge dent to their self-esteem and sense of worthlessness.

BUBBLE WRAPPED CHILDREN

"Will you agree to your child being adopted?" a question asked by lawyers and social workers. An uncontested adoption is easier and cheaper for them; quicker to implement, speeding the child's journey through placement and into an adoptive family. The child benefits by starting the therapeutic reparenting process earlier and the adoptive placement is more likely to survive. Should birth mum consent to the adoption?

"I don't' want to sign them because in years to come Sharon may feel I've given her away. I don't want Sharon's social worker and (family members) to say that I should sign so that Sharon can feel I like the family she is going to. It's not about that. I know that Sharon's adoption will happen anyway whether I sign or not and her adoptive family seem really nice, caring, warm, but I couldn't live with myself if I'd signed the papers. I wanted Sharon to know that I didn't want her to be adopted." Still Screaming P 44

The consent issue is very tricky for birth mothers. *"They felt that they were not worthy of their children and yet to consent to their adoption was rejecting them. This was a dilemma that caused recurrent pain even years later."* Still Screaming P45.

The current UK legal process of adversarial decision making in adoption is, to say the least, unhelpful. Basically in answer to the question "do you consent to your child being adopted?" a birth parent says either "yes" or "no". We need a third option which says, "Even though I don't want my child adopted, with the evidence being presented I know it is going to happen. I recognise this long drawn out legal process will harm my child, so with regret and sadness I agree to my child being adopted."

Emotional reaction
The following are common feelings, thoughts and emotional states voiced by birth mothers as a result of their children being removed:
- Δ Worthlessness
- Δ Humiliation
- Δ Powerlessness in the legal contest
- Δ Long-lasting feelings of sadness and depression that often magnified over time
- Δ Deep-seated guilt, especially if they believed they could have done more to prevent the adoption
- Δ Public judgement of social failure
- Δ Low self-esteem
- Δ Wariness of professional services – especially Social Services
- Δ Haunting and intrusive memories
- Δ Self-reproach and recriminations
- Δ Lifelong guilt which intensifies loss and provokes unworthiness

68

Although at this stage birth mothers are offered 'support' or 'counselling' from Social Services, they rarely take it. Understandably. They have no faith or trust in Social Services, why would they? "The f***ing SS" took their child away. Plus the personal weaknesses that contributed to her child being removed result in her being unable to access any help or support. So birth mothers are left with unresolved grief, floundering emotionally with a strong motivational driver to "reduce the pain". Mourning becomes "pathological" when adjustment to loss is not achieved.

This is why we need an independent support and counselling service for women who have their children permanently removed. They are grief stricken and continue to scream. Some are likely to have more children as a "cure" for their loss.

The extended grief cycle

The extended grief cycle below is an extended version of the classic five-stage Kubler-Ross grief cycle. The shock and testing stages have been added to her original model.

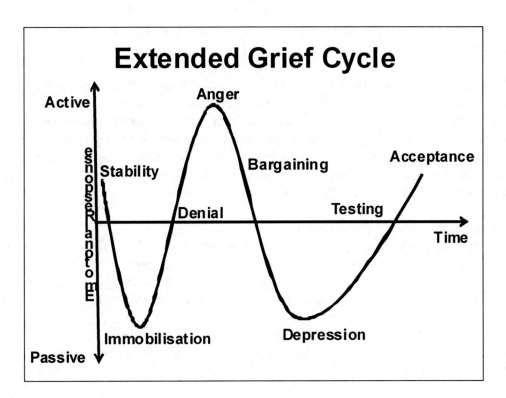

	Stage	Interpretation
1	Shock	Initial paralysis at hearing the bad news
2	Denial	Trying to avoid the inevitable
3	Anger	Frustrated outpouring of bottled-up emotion
4	Bargaining	Seeking in vain for a way out.
5	Depression	Final realization of the inevitable
6	Testing	Seeking realistic solutions
7	Acceptance	Finally finding the way forward

A common problem is that people get stuck in one phase. A person may become stuck in denial, never moving on from the position of not accepting the inevitable future. When it happens, they still keep on denying it, such as the person who has lost their job still going into the city only to sit on a park bench all day. Someone may be stuck in permanent anger (which is itself a form of flight from reality) or repeated bargaining. However, it's more difficult to get stuck in active states than in passivity. Getting stuck in depression is perhaps more common and is certainly a characteristic of many birth mothers.

Another trap is when a person moves on to the next phase without fully completing an earlier phase. So they flip-flop in cyclic loops that repeat previous emotion and actions. So when bargaining is not working, they may go back into anger or denial. Their behaviours are experienced by professionals dealing with birth mothers who appear inconsistent from one meeting to the next. This is also a way of avoiding the inevitable, because going backwards in time may seem to be a way of extending the time before the ghastly thing happens.

Longer term issues – the aftermath
The final stage of the grief process is "acceptance". Rarely do birth mothers get to that point. They are stuck in the cycle of grief. Maybe stuck at denial or cycling between anger and depression or immobilisation. Without good, appropriate, ongoing, independent support how can they process and resolve their grief?

Is it any wonder birth mothers self-harm, self-medicate with alcohol and drugs, take overdoses, become depressed, have psychological problems, bouts of fury or disconnect from everyday life?

Birth mothers report many ramifications of losing their child or children. Remember, some birth mothers lose a succession of children, their entire family or a subset of children. It's not uncommon for a birth mother to produce five or ten children who

70

over time who are all removed and placed in foster care or adopted. Consider the motivational factors in that situation and the challenges, not just for those birth mothers, but also the decision makers with whom they are involved. Now pause to consider the financial implications for social care planners and society from a birth mother who produces a baby every two years to alleviate the unresolved grief generated when the previous one was removed.

Having been discredited as a parent with the inevitable sense of worthlessness that brings, how can a birth mother care for existing or subsequent children? Can she do better next time? Will Social Services remove them? How can she protect herself?

How does a birth mother explain to neighbours and friends that her child was removed because "she is an unfit parent"? Moving house would alleviate that problem and stop triggering the memories associated with that home. Perhaps she needs to keep moving? Maybe she would prefer to stay in the flat with the memories and places she can remember playing with her son, but the neighbours have turned against her and she doesn't feel safe. Does she move to a new area, start afresh and deny she was ever a mother?

In almost every sphere of society, a mother losing her child is deemed a traumatic event. Miscarriages, still births, fatal childhood accidents or illnesses generally herald outpourings of sympathy and condolences. Yet this rarely is extended to mothers who lose their children to adoption or long-term fostering. In most quarters compassion and understanding is not extended to them, because they were "bad mothers". Even though the events and process that culminated in adoption constituting "trauma" (overwhelming emotions which they are unable to integrate), their loss is unmarked, their emotional state unresolved. Their own history probably deprived them of suitable role models and the opportunity to become "adequate parents" hence their ongoing status as "bad mothers".

Of course they keep screaming and trying to ease their pain. Wouldn't you? Sadly their strategies to numb the pain are often short-term and frequently self-destructive, possibly by abusing alcohol or drugs, falling into depression or abusive relationships or simply by having another baby. Constructive support is hard to find, particularly 24/7/365. However, as Chapter 16, Still Screaming, demonstrates, finding their child via Social Networking may be a great method to reduce the aching hurt, and Facebook can be accessed 24/7/365, so why wouldn't they take that route to resolve their trauma and grief?

BUBBLE WRAPPED CHILDREN

CHAPTER 8

TRAUMA

"Wounds that can't be seen are more painful than those that can be seen and healed by a doctor."
Nelson Mandela

Trauma pervades adoption, much of fostering and pockets of society.

The vast majority of problems adopted children face come not from the change in their legal status; it emanates from trauma; from experiencing the terrifying incidents, the absence of comfort when distressed, the feelings of anger, fear, disgust, rage, apathy and shame; the sense of worthlessness, hopelessness and helplessness. These building blocks of childhood trauma are the biggest issue in adoption.

It's not that the child was adopted, but the fact that the child was traumatised which needs to be addressed by adoptive parents, professionals and decision makers. Many children in foster care will also have experienced trauma, again their legal status is immaterial. It's what happened to them and how they interpreted their experience that's important.

Before looking at the impact of trauma during infancy, let's consider how trauma experienced in adulthood is recognised, classified and resolved and remembering that the removal of a child is a traumatic experience for most birth mothers.

PTSD: Post Traumatic Stress Disorder

Unresolved trauma is debilitating, it changes people's bodies, brains and lives. Although the human race has been exposed to trauma for many centuries, the formal classification of a specific disorder resulting from one or more catastrophic events and its effect on the mind, brain and body, is quite recent. The term Post Traumatic Stress Disorder first appeared in DSM III (Diagnostic and Statistical Manual of Mental Disorders) in 1980 and was last amended in 2000 (DSM IV TR). The next DSM update is in 2013 and amendments are under discussion.

In very simple terms PTSD occurs after a catastrophic event(s) outside the normal range of human existence and the individual experiences either overwhelming emotions which they are unable to integrate or a feeling they might die.

BUBBLE WRAPPED CHILDREN

Professor Gordon Turnbull views this as "a normal reaction to an abnormal event". He believes trauma is a "shatterer of assumptions". During the catastrophic event(s) such as rape, fierce combat, collecting body parts, car or air crash, witnessing the torture of your family, assault, an earthquake, or being a hostage, the body responds appropriately to that situation. It goes into hyper-aroused, survival mode. The older parts of the brain take over, blood flows to muscles in preparation for fleeing or fighting, the senses are heightened and emotions cascade through the individual.

The problem comes if the individual gets stuck with this appropriate reaction after the abnormal event has finished. The threat has gone, the world is safe, but the individual's body, mind and brain are locked into survival mode with no way of dissipating the energy associated with the trauma. Rather like the deep sea diver whose body has adapted to the high atmospheric pressure on the sea bed and needs to decompress slowly, after a shattering experience the trauma victim also needs to "decompress" safely, otherwise, sooner or later, they are more prone to develop PTSD.

PTSD is less likely to occur when an individual:
- Δ   Gets appropriate help and useful support soon after the event
- Δ   Regains control or takes action to reduce the sense of helplessness at the time
- Δ   Had secure attachments in childhood and high resilience
- Δ   Has time to "decompress" and debrief before re-entry into the 'real' world

The symptoms of PTSD typically include:
- Δ   Re-experiencing
  - ▲ flashbacks, intrusive thoughts, distressing dreams, uncontrolled reactions to external reminders of the event
- Δ   Avoidance of reminders of the event
  - ▲ Avoids places, people, no interest in life, detached, emotionally numb
- Δ   Hyper-arousal
  - ▲ Difficulty concentrating, sleeping, irritability, anger outbursts, hyper-vigilance, heightened startle response, jumpy.

To process PTSD an individual needs:
- Δ To feel safe; psychologically and physically
- Δ The opportunity to process and make sense the trauma
- Δ To create a coherent narrative and understand the whole experience

Trauma is not always a black and white issue. Some traumatic experiences do not lead to full blown PTSD; they may lead to partial symptoms. Sometimes a succession of events may result in a 'trauma response'.

74

Secondary Trauma is a recognised diagnosis for people who have maybe been supporting trauma victims, counsellors or members of the clergy can be victims. Living 24/7 with someone who has PTSD can also result in Secondary Trauma, so partners of military veterans with full-blown PTSD are susceptible. Being the adoptive or foster parent of traumatised children can also result in Secondary Trauma. An adult, or siblings, living with traumatised children where the potential of violence, an explosive temper outburst or being swore and shouted at is always present, will become hyper-vigilant and traumatised themselves. Kate Cairns writes about it as a recognisable by-product of being a foster carer. She noticed symptoms in herself and others. Me too: I know loss of humour is a big warning sign for me and others. I also know how living with long-term stress and trauma has impacted my body.

The body keeps score

It is becoming more widely recognised that trauma is stored in the body: primarily in the right brain, the implicit rather than explicit memory and specific parts of the limbic and reptilian brain. As these were more likely to have been activated and involved during the traumatic event, that's where the memories are stored; along with the associated feelings, emotions and sensory data which are not accessible with language,

"The body keeps score" is a phrase used by Bessel van der Kolk in his writing and teachings. As one of the foremost pioneers in the treatment of trauma for several decades, he has transformed both the thinking and practice of treating trauma. The Trauma Center in Boston, founded by him, offers therapy and support to adults and children, it also provides training, online resources and much information (www.traumacenter.org).

Other pioneers who recognised that trauma became locked in the body and influenced my thinking include the Americans Peter Levine, Pat Ogden and Babette Rothschild, each working to help clients safely discharge the trauma through various body-based therapies. In the UK, Professor Gordon Turnball's recent book "Trauma" unfolds the developments and thinking about trauma over the past few decades and includes this quote. *"The translation of a somatic experience – a body, sensory experience – in the right side of the brain into a left brain experience – a narrative, a verbal story – so that the patient can grasp it at a conscious level is what the treatment of PTSD is all about. In other words it is about the implicit becoming explicit."*

'The implicit becoming explicit' is my experience of working with adults who experienced trauma in childhood or as an adult. Using the extensive tools, thinking, processes and structure of NLP (Neuro-Linguistic Programming), I have been privileged to witness clients release traumatic memories and ugly experiences.

The processes for healing trauma with NLP follow the three basic principles for trauma healing in general. Firstly ensure the clients feels and stays safe (physically and psychologically) throughout. The trauma is then processed by viewing it from a very, very dissociated space to get the learnings which then help make sense of the experience. Finally the experience is 'recoded' so that the sensory triggers are unhooked from the memory.

Other methods which engage the right brain and are used successfully to melt and heal trauma include EFT (Emotional Freedom Technique, often called Tapping); EMDR (Eye Movement Desensitisation Reprocessing) which has its roots in NLP; and Somatic Experiencing, which incorporates body sensations into psychotherapy. I share this brief list so readers realise healing strategies exist. However, this is not the place for detailing the processes simply to offer hope and potential arenas for readers to pursue themselves.

Sensory triggers

Sensory triggers are a key component of PTSD. They could be sights, smells, sounds, tastes or feelings; within the body or external to it.

Maybe the smell of a council venue or the type of plastic chair may trigger nervousness or fear. For a birth mother it's possibly a reminder of numerous meetings with social workers which ultimately resulted in her child being removed. For the child it's a reminder of weekly contact with birth mum while he was being fostered, which was a deeply unsettling few months/years.

"The blue flashing lights on a police car just freak me out," said a victim of a major rail crash talking on the radio several years after the event. "I flip into panic mode instantly if I see any flashing blue lights. It could be while walking along the road or sitting in my front room."

She explained that while the rail carriage had been sliding along on its side after the derailment inside a tunnel, the darkness was broken by blue sparks as an electricity cable intermittently touched the rails. This illuminated the carnage around her. A series of stroboscopic still shots of an ongoing event were imbedded into her unconscious mind. (This strobe technique is used by film makers to grip audiences. Remember how effective it was in the last scene of Blackadder the Third as they went 'over the top').

The woman had been traumatised by the experience and the images haunted her. Blue flashing lights instantly took her back to that rail disaster and caused enormous anxiety and fear. The visual trigger of the flashing blue light connected to her implicit memory and caused the unconscious emotional outburst. A vivid example of a PTSD flashback.

For her, the triggers can be rationalised and understood, because she knows about the event and others can bear witness.

These responses are from the reptilian brain, the unconscious mind and uncontrollable, similar to a phobic response. At least with a phobia, the phobic knows the triggers and may know the root cause. Several years ago when walking along the pavement, my friend Sue unexpectedly veered away from me to avoid a pigeon. She saw the bird and was able to divert her path before terror took over.

Sue knew she had a phobic response to birds because, a bird had flown down the chimney flapped round her bedroom and into her cot, terrifying baby Sue. Later her parents could tell her about the event, so she understood the trigger, her response and the root cause. If the bird had flown back up the chimney and left no evidence, no one would have been able to explain Sue's hysterical fear of birds. Fortunately for Sue, someone could identify the cause. For children traumatised in infancy, by neglect or abuse, they don't know their triggers.

The neglected infant Joe may lie in darkness, smell curdled milk, have gripping hunger pains in his stomach, hear his mother's angry voice, feel his heart racing, the coldness of his feet. Those sensory experiences will be imprinted and could form the basis for a trauma triggered response later in life.

Developmental Trauma Disorder DTD (plus a metaphor)
The diagnosis of Post Traumatic Stress Disorder (PTSD) is rarely applied to children; their complex, disordered traumatic experience creates something different because they are still being formed when the damage occurs. Remember how "The Wall" becomes unstable when children's early needs are not met.

Metaphorically, if an adult has a traumatic event which results in PTSD, it's as if a car has been involved in a crash. The body work is damaged, and maybe the chassis is twisted. The event happened to a properly constructed machine which had previously functioned well.

However, if some trauma or disaster befalls the car during its manufacture, the effects are far more profound and often quite hidden. Maybe a spark plug is missing or only three wheel nuts were secured, maybe supposedly smooth surfaces inside compression chambers are pitted and cracked, maybe the exhaust partly vents through the air conditioning. Few of these features would be noticed on a gentle journey, none when looking from the outside at the stationary vehicle; but under stress, on a long motorway drive there is a distinct possible of spasmodic misfiring, sudden loss or surge of power, toxic fumes and a wheel falling off.

When trauma occurs during an infant's development, the damage impacts the entire body system. The brains wiring, (neurology), the body's fight/flight mechanisms (physiology), the child's inner world (psychological), at a cellular level construction is impacted by ingested chemicals (nutrition, drugs) and the body-generated chemicals like cortisol and adrenaline.

In their white paper, quoted below, the Complex Trauma Taskforce (part of the American National Child Traumatic Stress Network) – a group of world-famous respected trauma experts – used the term "Developmental Trauma Disorder" as the provisional name given to children who have complex trauma histories. Their intent is for Developmental Trauma Disorder to be included in DSM V due in 2013.

"Trauma has its most pervasive impact during the first decade of life and becomes more circumscribed, i.e., more like "pure" PTSD (Post Traumatic Stress Disorder), with age. The diagnosis PTSD is not developmentally sensitive and does not adequately describe the impact of exposure to childhood trauma on the developing child. Because multiply abused infants and children often experience developmental delays across a broad spectrum, including cognitive, language, motor, and socialization skills they tend to display very complex disturbances with a variety of different, often fluctuating, presentations."

"However, because there currently is no other diagnostic entity that describes the pervasive impact of trauma on child development these children are given a range of "comorbid" diagnoses, as if they occurred independently from the PTSD symptoms, none of which do justice to the spectrum of problems of traumatised children, and none of which provide guidelines on what is needed for effective prevention and intervention. By relegating the full spectrum of trauma-related problems to seemingly unrelated "comorbid" conditions, fundamental trauma-related disturbances may be lost to scientific investigation, and clinicians may run the risk of applying treatment approaches that are not helpful."

In essence they are saying we have to look at the whole child, including their traumatic experiences, to make sense of their world and to intervene effectively. Too many children receive diagnoses that simply ignore their traumatic history. The full article and lots more is at www.traumacenter.org

Bessel Van der Kolk says, *"The proposed diagnosis of Developmental Trauma Disorder is organised around the issue of triggered dysregulation in response to traumatic reminders, stimulus generalisation, and anticipatory organisation of behaviour to prevent the recurrence of the trauma effects."*

'Traumatic reminders' might be a sensory cue – a smell, a particular touch or sound (door bang, hand on knee) which sparks a spontaneous reaction (running out of the room, screaming, anger outburst) and behaviour is (unconsciously) organised to avoid echoing old hurts.

The smell of sour milk or having cold feet could trigger memories for Joe of lying neglected in that cot. The fear, shame, anger and disgust could burst into his physical being at any time. If as a teenager he is walking home from school during a heavy downpour with the wrong footwear, his reptilian brain engaged, his mood is probably ugly. He might provoke a fight, he might kick out verbally or physically or simply dissociate and appear to shut down. His behaviour is unpredictable because it is trauma triggered. Neither he nor his parents understand it.

How is this relevant to social networking?

Why does trauma relate to contact via Facebook, I hear you ask? Because both child and birth parents have unconscious sensory memories which will be triggered by the reconnection or just the possibility of linking. If that reconnection is not planned or facilitated, it will probably feel very unsafe for both parties, certainly hugely emotionally charged. Two vulnerable people will hook up without a safety net. The potential to confuse and retraumatize each other is huge. If it occurs during adolescence the problem is magnified because of the effect on the teenage brain.

BUBBLE WRAPPED CHILDREN

CHAPTER NINE

BRAIN & MEMORY

Trauma affects how the brain is created, develops and functions.

You know there are different parts of the brain and neuroscience is demonstrating that the environment, adult behaviour, stimulation, diet, fear, attachment patterns will affect how the neural networks in an infant, child, adolescent and adult develop. The science of epigenetics illustrates how some genes are switched on or off by internal processes, external stimuli and chemicals.

We know the brain is plastic. It can and will form new neural pathways and it will prune seldom used pathways, when that catchy phrase "neurons that fire together wire together" applies. This happens most in early infancy then as a toddler and young child, the next major pruning and rewiring process happens during adolescence.

Within this book I am not examining brain development or functioning except where it directly links to the impact of social networking on adoption. Hence the brain overview in this chapter is very, very brief and simple. For a deeper view the Child Trauma Academy (CTA) a not-for-profit organization, based in Houston, Texas headed by Dr Bruce Perry has much excellent material on its website, including free online tutorials. (www.childtraumaacademy.com).

Brain overview
There are several different models used to explain the brain's structure and functioning. Within this book I am using the Paul MacLean Triune model, because it is quite well known and simple. MacLean suggested that the brain is actually three brains in one, each developing as a response to evolutionary need.
  Δ   Reptilian Brain
      ▲ Oldest
      ▲ Brain stem and cerebellum
      ▲ Physical survival, maintenance and regulation of the body, digestion, breathing, circulation, balance,
      ▲ Instinctive responses
      ▲ 7 F's: fight, flight, freeze, fornicate, flop, feed, fart
      ▲ Least able to learn and adapt

- △ Limbic System
    - ▲ Hippocampus, amygdala, hypothalamus
    - ▲ Seat of emotion, most of nervous system,
    - ▲ Sensory experiences

- △ Neocortex
    - ▲ Newest part
    - ▲ Constitutes five-sixths of the brain
    - ▲ Language, abstract thought, imagination, consciousness, voluntary movement
    - ▲ Most able to learn and adapt

Children's brains

At birth the infant brain weighs about 400 gram, by one year it's about 1,000 grams, by late adolescence it's at its maximum – about 1,400 grams.
This increase is due to:

- △ Rapid generation of nerve cells (neurons) and supporting cells
- △ Connections (axons and dendrites) being formed between neurons
- △ Myelination. To ensure efficiency and speed of transmission the most frequently used connections are insulated with myelin, a fatty sheath, metaphorically like the plastic coating on an electrical wire or fibre optic cable.

Executive functioning skills begin in early infancy and should develop and improve sequentially throughout childhood and adolescence. As we saw in Chapter 4, these are vital for inhibition control, mindsight, empathy and thinking, which all impact educational progress and achievement.

However if external circumstances inhibit this development an individual may be left with some or all of their executive functioning skills stuck at a much younger age. The brain did not have the opportunity to grow and develop in an age appropriate way. Living with trauma, fear, abuse and neglect inhibits 'normal' brain pathways. The brain gets wired for living in a traumatic environment, because survival depends on it. Remember, neurons that fire together, wire together. Those connections become myelinated, hence more efficient. This brain is wired to respond to trauma, so executive functioning myelination in the neo cortex often may be significantly reduced.

Adolescents' brains

Our own eyes notice the physical growth spurts which puberty brings. Puberty also brings a brain growth spurt. During adolescence and early adulthood another major pruning and rewiring of the brain takes place, affecting about 15% of the brain. Sometimes it's as if their brains go 'offline'. "Blame my Brain: the amazing teenage brain revealed," by Nicola Morgan is useful reading for adults and teenagers as it explains the developmental process and some behavioural ramifications.

This has, in the past, been a pivotal time for adoptees to rewire their brains because they are in a safer place with adults who can parent therapeutically. They can fill in some of the 'wall' gaps; learn self regulation, new perspectives, impulse control etc while also exerting their teenage independence. It's a difficult balance and often a challenging time for an adoptive family.

Implicit and explicit memory

We used to think that babies and infants would not remember their experiences. This was simply because most people try to recall experiences with words. Even now many people think adopted children won't remember anything about their birth family or early traumatic experiences. I've often heard people say about my children, *"Oh but they've been with you so long; the early stuff can't matter now, they won't remember it"*. *WRONG!* So very, very wrong. This stuff matters because until it is understood, resolved and healed; the infancy trauma stored in the body is triggered by sensory memories and can't be accessed through words.

Daniel J Seigal in The Developing Mind explains the difference between implicit and explicit memory
- Δ   Implicit (early) memory: mental models, behaviours, images and emotions
- Δ   Explicit (late) memory: facts, events and autobiographical consciousness

Unlike explicit memory, implicit memory is present at birth.

"Implicit memories when retrieved are not thought to carry with them the internal sensation that something is being recalled... Implicit memory involves parts of the brain that do not require conscious processing during encoding and retrieval... we act, feel and imagine without recognition of the influence of past experience on our present reality".

"Implicit memory relies on brain structures that are intact at birth and remain available throughout life... Including the amygdala and other limbic regions for emotional memory, the basal ganglia and motor cortex for behavioural memory and the perceptual cortices for perceptual memory."
(Dan Seigal)

Filing System Metaphor

Memory storage for the explicit memory is rather like a huge filing system where the content is neatly recorded on index cards. These cards have detailed classifications which can easily be found because there is an efficient, detailed, cross referencing system. Each event can be filed under many different headings and so easily accessed. With explicit memory there is an organised system.

The implicit memories are more like a heap. Events are recorded on cards, but the cards have no headings or titles. There is no coherent classification, just a huge jumble of memory cards which are dumped into a mountainous, disorganised pile.

Memory formation, storage and access is a huge topic. I am touching only the facets relevant to children reconnection with birth family i.e. the early implicit memories and the resultant embedded emotional triggers or cues.

In our first year, we only have implicit memory with autobiographical memory starting around 18-24 months. So, for many children, adopted from the care system, the vast majority of their early experiences would be within the birth family or foster care. (Average age at time of adoptive placement is four.

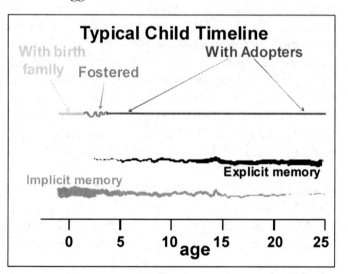

Traumatised children will have ghastly events and terrifying memories stored within their implicit memory which have sensory triggers; sounds feelings, smells, images, heart rate, and temperature. The list of potential sensory triggers is endless.

As we saw in the last chapter, for an adopted child seeing or hearing members of their birth family will trigger all sorts of emotional and sensory response which would be hard to fathom.

An adopter's anecdote

"Some years back, I was sitting round the kitchen table having a lovely time with my kids, over juice, tea and cake. Something happened and I started laughing and laughing – almost hysterically. Once I regained my composure it became clear that my ten-year-old daughter had shifted from a happy, contented, relaxed state to a hyper vigilant, fearful, anxious state. The other children aged seven, eleven and twelve were fine and unaffected.

"After some discussion and considerable self-awareness from my daughter, we established that my laughter had triggered an unconscious fear that the mirth would be followed by a slide into depression, collapsing or an angry rage. My daughter's birth mother abused alcohol. The 'high' phase would, all too often, have been followed by scary scenes. My laughter triggered her unconscious response, conditioned through experience for her own survival. A raucous laughing mother meant 'BEWARE'.

"We worked that one out. How many other unconscious sensory triggers had caused her to be angry, scared, or frozen?"

Contradictory evidence

One of the problems for adopted children is the presence of conflicting evidence. The adults around them saying "it's okay", "don't worry"; yet their body shouts a contradictory message. Data from their implicit memory is warning that danger is present or close. How does that child resolve the clash between his internal and external cues? Whom or what does he trust – himself or others? Does he rely on his implicit memory and unconscious senses or the adults around him? Does he follow his gut instinct? What can he trust?

BUBBLE WRAPPED CHILDREN

CHAPTER TEN

TRUST, TRANSITIONS AND DRAMA

"One ounce of pre-frame is worth a pound of reframe."
Judith De Lozier

Trust is at the heart of relationships; their creation, growth, development and endings.

Adopted and foster children frequently have their trust and faith in adults broken, which has consequences.

'Trust' is rarely defined in the context of child development, child care proceedings, decision making or contact issues. My dictionary defines trust as "confident belief in or reliance on the character, ability, strength, honesty etc of somebody or something". Trust, or lack of it, is important in every relationship you ever have; whether, brief, superficial, intense or prolonged; personal or professional.

Trust is a key factor in:
- Δ   the infant attachment cycle
- Δ   when professionals make decisions about a child's future
- Δ   parenting generally and especially when caring for traumatised children
- Δ   the child's perspective on their birth family
- Δ   establishing "the truth" about their past for maltreated children
- Δ   planning or conducting any form of contact
- Δ   therapy

Trust model
 A model for trust currently used in the business world is useful. The source is an article by Charles H. Green "Trust in Business: The Core concepts" found at www.trustedadvisor.com this incorporates material from The Trusted Advisor (Maister, Galford & Green 2000) and 'Trust based selling", McGraw-Hill

The equation is self-explanatory and has applications in many arenas. Do you trust the workman fitting your new boiler, do you trust the TV weather forecast, do you trust your partner to do the washing, and do you trust your child to cross the road safely? Your answer will be evidence based; how well did they fulfil their task on previous occasions?

Trust Equation

$$T = \frac{C + R + I}{S}$$

T = Trust
C = Credibility
R = Reliability
I = Intimacy
S = Self Interest

Trust Questions

Credibility: Can you do what you say you will do?
Reliability: Will you do what you say you will do?
Intimacy: How comfortable do I feel with you?
Self Interest:: What's in it for you?

Trusted Advisor: Maister, Galford & Green

The chart below focuses on each component within the context of contact issues.

Trust Components	Business/Sales definition	Some questions relevant to adoption, contact and connection via Facebook
Credibility	Words spoken and historical proof	Do we believe them? Do they have the knowledge and /or skills required? What evidence is there for this belief? Are they capable of this behaviour?
Reliability	Actions taken and track record	Are they consistent? Can they sustain this behaviour over time? What % of the time did or do they honour commitments?
Intimacy	Safety or security we feel when entrusting someone with something	Do I feel safe with you? Do you trigger a deep-seated fear in me?
Self-Orientation/ Self-Interest	Refers to focus of person in question	What's in it for them? What do they want from connecting? Is this for them or someone else?

Contact while a child is being fostered

One of the beauties of this model when applied to any contact arrangements is that amongst other things:

Δ the criteria can be objectively calibrated, recorded and used as evidence

Δ it is transparent and can be shared with birth parents

Δ it allows for individuals and circumstances to change over time

Δ it takes account of an individual's feelings and emotional state

Δ it acknowledges unconscious, gut feelings that can't be vocalised

Δ it adds mindsight, by considering the other person's perspective and possible motivations

Δ a track record or audit trail of reliability is available to all

Δ patterns can be seen, trends monitored, predictions made

Δ contact sessions between a child in foster care and their birth parent(s) can be recorded. The number of sessions attends, misses, lateness is objective evidence of reliability. It can be used by an adopted child in later life story work to help make sense of their experience.

Goodbye visits

After the final legal decisions confirming adoption as the plan, a "farewell visit" is often arranged between a child and the birth parent(s). Frequently the child does not understand the purpose of this specific meeting which seems no different to any others. Being told the purpose does not equal comprehension for a child, or often an adult. Many children do not realise they will not be seeing their birth parent(s) again. From the child's perspective, during his eighteen months in foster care, he has been seeing his mum maybe every week or fortnight. What makes this particular visit any different? The pattern seems the same to him.

For the birth parent(s), the goodbye visit has a very different feel. For them it is hugely emotional, painful and harrowing. They may dissociate or become highly emotional. Birth parents may also not fully believe this is a final "goodbye". They may believe it is "au revoir", literally until we meet again, a temporary parting and that reunification will occur in the future.

Even though these occasions are "supervised" by social workers, birth parents frequently tell their children that they will find them and be reunited. It's whispered in ears during hugs; it's told on a trip to the toilet or written on paper slipped into a pocket. This may shock or surprise some readers, but why wouldn't they? These birth parents are screaming inside and their pain will ease on reunification. Of course they want their children to know they will be reunited; and reunited asap. Mothers use phrases such as: "I will always love you"; "I think about you all the time"; "You are my little princess"; "Don't forget me". They may ask the child "Will you always love me?", "Will you promise to find me when you are older?" Of course the child will say yes, make that commitment and feel compelled to honour it.

Birth parents will tell children other things. Suzi, a four-year-old was told by her birth mother "I want to tell you a secret. Mummy has a baby inside her tummy". A year later Suzi shared this 'worry' with her adoptive mother. It took weeks before clarification of the deceit could be established adequately for Suzi. It had been a big fat lie. The birth mother had been in prison for so long that pregnancy was simply impossible; however Suzi spent 20% of her life holding that 'secret' and worrying about her birth mother. Suzi also did not know she would not see her birth mother again: that 'news' was broken by her adoptive mother. Might Suzi subsequently believe that her adoptive mother had "stolen her" from her birth mother? It's possible. How much would or could Suzi trust either mother?

A decade later when birth mum contacts Suzi through a social networking site and they start texting each other, what might the outcome be? Will birth mum admit to lying about the pregnancy? What if she denies that lie and the reason for her prison sentence?

How many times have you accepted information at face value, because you desperately wanted to believe that person, even though deep down you knew it was suspect? Maybe you could not entertain the thought that that specific individual might lie to you: maybe it would invalidate the relationship, maybe it would mean other 'facts' were false. This data could rock your world. What or whom do you believe? Yourself or another? Accept a hard truth, shatter a long-held dream or hold onto a fantasy? These are the choices facing maltreated children when reviewing their past.

Hello. I'll be taking care of your child

Unless there is thought to be a major safety issue, prospective adopters often have a one off meeting with the birth parents, its generally just the birth mother. Although a scary prospect for all, it is generally felt to be "a good thing". It punctures some myths the adopters may have after reading the Child Placement Report and the child's chronology. Photographs of the two sets of parents together are normally added to life story books.

Discussions are quite superficial; the real communication tends to be non-verbal. Adopters are warned not to share identifying facts which might reveal their location but to connect and find common ground or hear stories about the child. Promises about letterbox contact might be confirmed. In effect, future doors are opened.

However, whether this is a trustworthy, honest situation is questionable. Possibly the underlying message the birth parent hears is "I will look after your son until you can again". No adopter is going to say outright, "he is now my son not yours, so stay away from him," or, "you hurt him so much I will ensure he hears all the dreadful things you let happen." Because adopters have empathy, mindsight and decent executive functioning, they are generally sympathetic to the sad, unhappy woman sitting before them. The birth mother perspective and objectives may be very different. She may simply be waiting until she can reconnect to her son.

At this stage the adopters often see the birth mother as primarily a victim. A victim of her circumstances, her upbringing, her poor choices and her lack of support. The adopters may also feel some guilt, after all, on some level, they are taking this woman's child(ren) away from her.

The Drama Triangle

With its roots in Transactional Analysis, the Drama Triangle is a neat little model which can highlight three habitual roles that can be played out in a relationship with another or with oneself.

It is another "game people play".

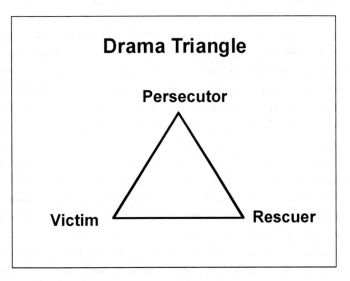

Δ	Victim	person who behaves as or is treated as "the victim"
Δ	Persecutor	person who pressurises, coerces or forces the victim
Δ	Rescuer	person who intervenes because ostensibly they want to help

However, each "role" is serving the selfish needs of the participants either consciously or unconsciously. Each role has payoffs, benefits and positive by-products for each corner of the triangle which can create co-dependency and dysfunctional relationships.

BUBBLE WRAPPED CHILDREN

When a child is removed, the social workers perceive themselves as Rescuers; the child is seen as the Victim and the birth parent the Persecutor. However the birth parent views herself the Victim, because social workers are persecuting her while she strives to protect and 'rescue' her child. As this situation demonstrates, each role creates the circumstances whereby a person can feel justified in their feelings or actions or wishes. However these are a substitute for a more genuine and mature emotional response which would be more appropriate.

Learned helplessness

Another scenario which often occurs within the adoption and fostering world is the "learned helplessness" and "victimhood" of many birth mothers. Particularly those who grew up in the care system or into a family where there has been intergenerational low achievement, dysfunctionality and chaos which required regular professional intervention (Social Services, police, courts or health).

These birth mothers who have 'learned helplessness' are stuck in victim mode. They will select partners who initially seem to offer 'rescuing', but that can become manipulative, controlling behaviour and transform into persecution, evidenced by anger, jealousy or domestic violence. For these birth mothers the characteristics of their partners generally remain the same, the name and face change but the behavioural patterns are simply repeated.

People with "learned helplessness" attract rescuers, one after another, dozens in succession. 'Rescuers' could be social workers, neighbours, housing officers, family members, solicitors, friends, casual acquaintances, therapists, police officers, doctors or civil servants managing their benefit claims. Many of these people feel very sorry for the poor woman and her ghastly circumstances. They may offer advice, complete forms, offer tea and sympathy, give money, suggest parenting or healthy living strategies, provide babysitting, lend money, buy food. However if after a while when their assistance makes no difference, frustration will set in. Professionals may stay involved but relationships with neighbours and friends often breakdown and can become acrimonious, as these casual acquaintances shift to the 'perpetrator' role.

Many people with learned helplessness have developed excellent strategies to attract and manipulate assistance from 'rescuers'. Their superficial behaviour and manner is often endearing and believable. They may use tears, a baby voice, plead, promise to change, ask for your help, say no one else understands them like you do, tell you dreadful stories about their past with just enough truth to be credible.

Remember that members of the caring professions do just that: they care. Helping people is their motivation and keeps them in that job. Hence there may be a tendency to slide into the rescue role. It's particularly easy when dealing with displays of learned helplessness, because the victim's gratitude or tiny behavioural changes gives satisfaction to the rescuer.

What if, in a social work department with a high staff turnover, the failure to change goes unnoticed because no social worker stays with her long enough to see the pattern of broken promises and failures? Is the "learned helplessness" noticed by the system or in supervision?

Over-optimism and trust

One of the findings from Lord Laming's report about "Baby Peter" was that social workers were "overly optimistic." This tendency was also noted in the 2011 Munro review.

My experience is that it applies to a much wider range of people including adopters, foster carers, social workers, health visitors, teachers and therapists. Not all of them, but some. Optimism is a useful personal characteristic or quality that helps us get through tough times. It's a motivator. However in the professional world we should be calibrating, measuring and establishing solid evidence for the views we hold and decision we reach.

It is difficult for social workers working with a struggling family. On the one hand they need and want the family to trust them, so intimacy is required. Intimacy is very personal. On the other hand they have to judge the family and make life changing decisions on whether or not to remove their children. After a few months or years of working with a family and investing much emotional energy into them, it is hard for the social worker to make tough decisions objectively, without robust criteria. That is where "over-optimism" sprouts.

Over-optimism also occurs within adoptive and foster families. It is sometimes hard facing up to the brutal truth that the children who live with you lie, have limited executive functioning or were sexually abused. It is painful to realise your son deliberately stole your purse or favourite jumper just because he was upset and angry with the world.

The trust equation gives parents solid criteria for stepping back and taking an honest objective view of their children. Without this, as foster or adoptive parents we can't give them what they <u>need</u>. We can't see or fill those gaps in their wall.

Children's behaviour is their vocabulary and must be interpreted accordingly.

I have witnessed adoptive parents who have repeatedly ignored behavioural signs and signals over years. They disregarded all the clues that the maltreatment suffered in infancy had damaged their child. Because these parents would not face up to the truth, their children did not get the therapeutic reparenting or adoption support they needed, while the challenging behaviour continued and often magnified.

Adopter preparation

Many adults become adopters as a result of infertility. That was my route. There may already be a sense of failure, a feeling that your body (or your partners) has let you down. You have already experienced a loss. This is a potential benefit for an adopter because, assuming you have processed that grief, you can have more empathy with the losses suffered by a child. However some adopters feel they have more to prove as a parent, which this can lead to blinkered thinking and a disregard of evidence or outstanding therapeutic reparenting.

For an adopter to accept that their new child does not trust them (or anyone else) is hard, unless they have understood what maltreatment does to a child. Too often prospective adopters have not grasped the difference between parenting normal or challenging children and parenting traumatised children.

Some professionals think that prospective adopters will be 'put off' if they heard the gruesome truth. Some might. That's fine, because maltreated children need parents who can hold their hideous history, embrace their pain and love them despite their presenting behaviour. They also need parents who can fight for them, who will demand action from the school, the local authority, the health service and the community to help heal their child.

Without the transition from "I want my own healthy baby" to "I will take on someone else's damaged child" prospective adopters are simply not equipped for the first step in a long and difficult journey. The optimistic view that "love is enough" is delusional.

PART 2: POST ADOPTION

*"In the vast majority of cases,
adopted children and their families will require
health and education support for life."*

Dr Mary Mather
Chair BAAF Health Advisory Group 2000-05
Medical Director: Parents for Children

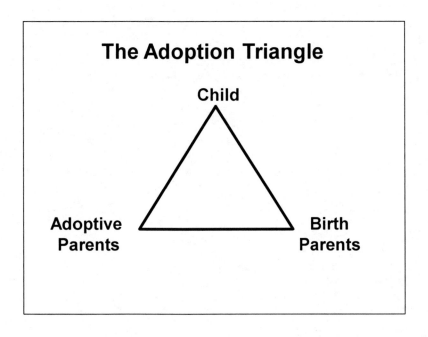

The Adoption Triangle

Child

Adoptive
Parents

Birth
Parents

BUBBLE WRAPPED CHILDREN

CHAPTER ELEVEN

WHY THERAPEUTIC REPARENTING?

Parenting is probably the most difficult task an adult undertakes and yet it is the role for which most of us are least trained. Although most mothers attend antenatal classes, there is rarely the equivalent educative and supportive organisation when our child is two, five, nine, thirteen, seventeen or twenty-one. Many people tend to parent how they were parented unless they make a very conscious effort to do it differently.

In the average book shop there are far more 'how to parent a baby' books than books about middle childhood or teenage parenting strategies. This may reflect parental anxiety at their lack of skills and experience when the baby is new, and by the time the child is four, eight, twelve or sixteen, parents feel more confident. Even though the understanding of the range of developmental milestones and 'what is normal' behaviour at a certain age is frequently patchy for many parents, most parents muddle through and raise 'okay' kids.

As we saw in previous chapters, traumatised children had a very different type of parenting in their early years. Before we examine what traumatised children need to overcome the legacy of toxic parenting, it is worth benchmarking what constitutes excellent parenting. There are many model and theories, plus various TV programmes apparently showing 'wild children' transforming quickly just with behaviour modification strategies.

One approach based on neuroscience and psychology is that advocated by Dr Dan Siegel, author of "The Developing Mind", in which the author links neurobiology, attachment, emotion and interpersonal relationships. This background gives him credibility and a solid methodology which can be used for 'normal' children and also maps across to traumatised children, hence its use here.

One conscious "normal" parenting approach
In 'Parenting from the Inside Out', Dan Seigel and Mary Hartzell suggest five anchor points for understanding this link between the neuroscience of the child's developing mind and interpersonal connection. The components are mindfulness, lifelong learning, response flexibility, mindsight and joyful living. I've added some specific behaviours which would demonstrate the trait, because as we have seen previously, their absence is the often the trademark of toxic parents.

△ **Mindfulness** occurs when we are fully present in the now, aware of our own thoughts and feelings and open to those of others. We connect fully to another when interacting with them. Being mindful as a parent means you "purposefully choose your behaviour with your child's wellbeing in mind" and ensures you are mentally present for them.

△ **Lifelong learning** is a trait that allows us to examine our current behaviour, beliefs and issues from the past and modify or adapt our thinking in the light of new evidence or learnings. Parenting offers us a chance to re-examine our own leftover childhood issues. Seigal states "if you approach such challenges as a burden, parenting can become an unpleasant chore". If we see parenthood as a learning opportunity, in which to grow and develop, we will nurture curiosity in ourselves and our children.

△ **Response flexibility** "is the ability to sort through a wide variety of mental processes such as impulses, ideas and feelings, and come up with a thoughtful non-automatic response". This can be tricky when you are tired, angry or your mind is elsewhere, when a knee-jerk reaction is more likely. This type of behavioural flexibility requires impulse control and the ability to delay gratification and avoid the quick fix. The ability to pause, breath, stay calm and consider options is necessary.

△ **Mindsight** "is the ability to perceive our own minds and the minds of others". Mindsight involves seeing below the superficial presenting behaviour of the child, into the possible root cause and motivation, using the non-verbal signals to understand the internal processes in operation. A child who starts crying may be upset, hungry, sad, angry, tired, wanting attention, hurt, scared, feel unloved or in pain. A sensitive parent will be able to appraise the situation and offer appropriate action and comfort.

△ **Joyful living** "Enjoying your child and sharing in the awe of discovering what it means to be alive, to be a person in a wondrous world, is crucial for the development of your child's positive sense of self." Simply being with children, maybe kicking a ball in the park, reading a story, laughing at their jokes, sharing their achievements, big and small, cooking together and generally letting them know you enjoy their company and choose to spend time with them.

Children who, from birth, grew up with parents who frequently exhibit these characteristics are likely to develop secure attachments, a strong sense of self with positive beliefs about themselves and the world. Although there will be difficult moments, times when these children test boundaries, these adults will parent proficiently. Their children are likely to develop into confident, competent individuals with high self-esteem, high empathy, high resilience and "well wired" brains.

The story for traumatised children is very different. We know their brains will have been wired differently, their sense of self and belief system reflecting the negative, dangerous world they inhabited. To complicate matters they have protected themselves with bubble wrap, distorting our view of them while their vista is blurred by these layers.

Entry into foster care

Having been removed from their toxic parents, these children enter the foster care system. They may have one, several or numerous foster families. Each family functions differently. Every bed will look, feel and smell unfamiliar. The foster mother might be thin, fat, tall, short, loud, quiet, left-handed or right-handed. There might be dogs, cats or rabbits. There might be other children or none. Even if every foster family is "brilliant": each and every move stirs up anxiety, fear, sadness, anger, and uncertainty in the child. Pause for a moment and reflect on the multitude of sensory triggers being installed alongside those negative feelings. The creaking of a door, the wafting aroma of sizzling bacon, a specific TV programme theme, the smell of bleach or cat food, a deep dog bark, the feel of cotton wool, Christmas carols, sand, cold water. The list is endless and unknown.

On occasions, reunification with the birth family is attempted. Sometimes for just days, maybe weeks, even months. However, frequently this fails; the child is removed and placed in yet another foster home. This process may repeat numerous times so birth parents have the opportunity to demonstrate, beyond doubt, whether they can parent adequately.

The removal itself will involve several social workers, possibly the police, probably with birth family members strongly objecting. There is a cacophony of sound, screaming, shouting and crying which partially drowns out the radio blasting out "We will Rock You" while Joe is physically removed from the arms of Emma, his hysterical mother. This ugly scene imprints deep sensory memories for both Joe and Emma.

Trauma triggered behaviour

Fast forward a few years and whenever Queen's classic tune is played both Joe and Emma could become upset or angry. Neither knows why. Neither realise that this particular song was the trigger for their change of state. The distinctive drum rhythm alone might be enough to spark an unconscious reaction.

What if Joe was adopted by rock fans who liked playing Queen's music in the car?

BUBBLE WRAPPED CHILDREN

This exemplifies the difficulties of parenting traumatised children. You never know when their current behaviour is linked to a past trauma or is related to current events. Joe and his adoptive father could be driving to football practice discussing the goal Joe scored last week and how Joe plans to score another in today's match. The atmosphere is light; they are laughing and chatting happily, sometimes singing along to the records on the radio. At the opening drumbeat of We will Rock You, his dad turns up the radio volume, starts singing, inviting Joe to join in. Joe explodes, screams he doesn't want to play football, that he hates the team and his dad. In a nanosecond, Joe has shifted from calm to hyper-aroused and angry.

We have the benefit of observing from the outside and can recognise what triggered that outburst from Joe. Sadly neither Joe nor his dad can.

Understanding that an adopted or foster child's behaviour may be trauma triggered is a keystone to parenting a traumatised child. Without it their behaviour makes no sense. Holding the constant possibility of "trauma triggered behaviour" in your mind makes sense of what appears to be their nonsensical behaviour and is essential for any adult living or working with such a child.

Therapeutic reparenting

While parenting traumatised children requires mindfulness, lifelong learning, response flexibility, mindsight and joyful living, it also needs more. Much, much more.

This book is not covering "how to parent traumatised children". That is an entire book in itself. However an overview of the principles is necessary and useful. Readers will find that the term "developmental parenting" is used in some quarters including Bruce Perry. I am using the term therapeutic reparenting because it distinguishes both the developmental gaps i.e. holes in the wall and the trauma component.

Therapeutic reparenting differs from 'normal' parenting in two distinct ways.

Δ   **Re**parenting = filling in the development gaps
Δ   **Therapeutic** parenting = repairing the damage

Therapeutic parenting

Therapeutic parenting is parenting with a historical perspective, honouring the pain, suffering and trauma the child has experienced and helping the child make sense of their experience. For example:

Δ Recognising that anniversaries are difficult

Δ Holding a safe space (literally and metaphorically) when a child discloses what Uncle Fred did.

Δ Maintaining a calm controlled manner all the time; shouting retraumatizes the child. Easy to say, difficult to maintain 100% of the time, almost impossible without good ongoing support.

Δ Seeing food hoarding as a method the child uses (unconsciously) to keep themselves safe

Δ Realising that a "time out" is interpreted as rejection, so a "time in" is a better strategy.

Reparenting

Reparenting necessitates the adult seeing and responding to "the age of the current behaviour" and recognising which bricks in the child's "needs wall" require repair. For example:

Δ A twelve-year-old child, neglected as an infant who has difficulty controlling his emotions may need a cuddle every time he is upset, which you can do at home but around his classmates a finger squeeze, hair ruffle or wink might be more appropriate.

Δ With her permission, being spoon fed can be nurturing for an adopted seventeen-year-old who is feeling tired or ill. A tiny repair to her 'wall'.

Δ Often adopters have to "think toddler" when their teenager or young adults behaves "bizarrely".

Δ Taking something without asking in a three-year-old is normal behaviour, they have little impulse control; in a fifteen-year-old it's classified as stealing, yet many adopted children at fifteen have poor impulse control (part of executive functioning skills) and take things without permission.

Δ A child who didn't learn to socialise will struggle in school to make friends and not understand why hitting is not okay. Sensitive reparenting teaches a ten-year-old to share.

PLACE Model

Dan Hughes PhD, a clinical psychologist, practices "Dyadic Developmental Psychotherapy", a treatment approach to trauma, loss and neglect based on attachment and PTSD principles. He works with fostered and adopted children and their families in the USA. He also teaches internationally and has delivered many training courses throughout the UK, including several levels of "Trauma and the

Road to Recovery". Hughes was influenced by Milton Erickson, the acclaimed hypnotherapist who had been modelled by the developers of NLP. Hence, at times, I found myself on familiar ground when attending his trainings and implementing his strategies. The NLP principles of rapport, sensory acuity, behavioural flexibility and being outcome orientated pervade his work. Along with Family Futures, who incorporate his principles in their therapy and training, Dr Hughes has touched thousands of families who parent traumatised children.

The therapeutic model taught by Dan Hughes promotes an attitude that encourages parents and therapists to be:

- Δ **P**layful
- Δ **L**oving
- Δ **A**ccepting
- Δ **C**urious
- Δ **E**mpathetic

As we will see in the next chapter, the need and role of 'acceptance' and 'curiosity' in the parental tool kit becomes vital when children are processing painful episodes from their life before placement.

Adoptive parenting brings isolation

Therapeutic reparenting is often counter-intuitive. Because, quite rightly, adopters don't share their children's history with people, their parenting style is often criticised. Adopted children may need very firm boundaries and lots of nurturing. Their behaviour can be very challenging (stealing, lying, acting out, 'very naughty', aggressive, self-harming, violent), and other parents in the playground are often quick to judge. This can be isolating and distressing for the adoptive parents.

Secondary trauma is a potential by-product of living with traumatised children. One adoptive mother Hilary, told me about her thirteen-year-old daughter who was very angry, stole, lied and was highly unpredictable. After one particularly challenging day when her daughter threatened to kill her, Hilary reflected while nestled under the duvet. "She could get a knife from the kitchen and stab me during the night... Ah well; that will solve the problem one way or another." An exhausted Hilary rolled over and went to sleep.

I shared that story with a group of adoptive mothers, who laughed and recounted similar thoughts. Hilary could not share that story with 'normal parents', their eyes would have popped out. Neither could she share the history of sexual abuse which was the source of her daughter's rage. Despite this, Hilary was refused funding for therapy and the family was left to cope alone.

Support from other adoptive parents is vital. Sharing experiences with a peer group is known to be useful and healing. It is one of the strategies frequently used by Professor Turnbull as part of his PTSD treatment programme. However, with adoption it requires genuine knowledge of the underlying trauma and attachment issues and an intrinsic 'knowing' in the muscle of what living with traumatised children is really like. That's why adopter-to-adopter support is vital. Adopters together will share painful stories, advice, thoughts, support and hurt with humour and compassion in a way that rarely happens when "professionals" are present.

Ideally, therapeutic reparenting continues throughout childhood, adolescence and early adulthood, so that the positive healthy brain rewiring can continue. The parents need to hold a safe space for the child.

During adolescence when pulling away from your family, identity issues and rebelling are part of the teenage job description. Holding that safe space in adolescence is very tricky for many adoptive families. Intrusions from the birth family via Facebook can and do shatter that safe space. It also brings in falsehoods.

CHAPTER TWELVE

THE TRUTH, THE WHOLE UNSPEAKABLE TRUTH AND NOTHING BUT THE TRUTH

"It is difficult to grow up as a psychologically healthy adult if one is denied access to one's own history. The very fact that adults hesitate to share with a child information about his or her past implies that it was so bad that the young person won't be able to cope with it.
Whatever the past was, the child lived through it and survived.
He or she has already demonstrated survival skills."
Vera Fahlberg. A Child's Journey Through Placement 1994

My belief is that children need 100% of the information about their history however disgusting. As previous chapters have demonstrated, they already know it. It is stored sensually in the body/mind and contained in their implicit and explicit memory.

The words used in court, police or social work reports; photos or the personal narrative of a trustworthy source who can 'bear witness', simply confirm the child's intrinsic data. The child's understanding and interpretation of the information is critical to their self-image and belief system. If aspects of the past are ignored or considered "too awful to share", shame will pervade the child.

Obviously the child needs supportive assistance to process their history and the content has to be age appropriate. In essence the child needs to gently be taken through the learning cycle to process the tough stuff. They have already had the experience, now they can safely review the events, draw some conclusions and pragmatically decide how to use those new perspectives. Without external facilitation and support the child will not be able to process their past, so have no possibility of updating beliefs or changing their internal working model.

"What is shareable is bearable."
Dan Seigal

Jigsaw metaphor

The information has to be age-appropriate; what you tell a five-year-old is different to the content shared with a nine, thirteen or eighteen-year-old. Imagine you were buying them each a jigsaw of a coastal scene. The five-year-old may have a jigsaw with fifteen large pieces depicting sand, sea, sky, a red boat, a sandcastle, green bucket and purple spade. The eighteen-year-old might have a thousand tiny pieces, depicting all those plus rocks, caves, people, fishing nets, trees, cliffs, a waterfall, paths, grass, windbreaks, towels, beach huts, clouds and breakwaters: a much more complex picture. The nine and thirteen-year-old respectively would maybe have an eight piece and three-hundred-and-fifty piece puzzle, the picture becoming more detailed each time.

Each time by first finding the edges, boundaries would be established, and the overall shape of the puzzle is visible. Then maybe sort the pieces into groups "this looks like sky", "here is some beach", to outline and systematise the content. This process performed in small manageable chunks would build on previous knowledge, understanding and picture from the earlier bigger pieced jigsaws. Learning would be facilitated by putting in breaks and pauses to assimilate information along with the opportunity to step away from the detail and see the developing picture from a distance. Hence reflection, theorising and pragmatism are all built into the learning process. At all times the child must feel safe.

With this type of approach there would be no major surprises or secrets for the child as they matured, simply more detail and a deeper understanding. The protective bubble wrap is gently peeled away allowing the child a more accurate and empowering view of themselves and the world. As the bubble wrap drops away, rather like upgrading a television, the picture is in high definition and the sound sharper.

Knowing at five that "Uncle Fred was a bad man, who did naughty things" can gradually develop into "Uncle Fred was probably a paedophile, who was imprisoned for filming sexual acts inflicted on children". Knowing at five that "my birth father hurt me and it was not my fault" might culminate at eighteen in reading police and hospital reports detailing the injuries sustained and accepting: "my father was a psychopath whose abuse of me was the consequence of zero empathy and mental instability fuelled by drugs and alcohol. It is not a genetic trait or inherited condition so I can choose to behave differently. I will practice mindsight, empathy, compassion and control my temper. I do not want to follow in his footsteps."

Life story work or rose-tinted glasses?
What if every traumatised child had the opportunity to process, learn and grow with such congruence? Sadly it's the exception rather than the rule. For most adopted children their "life story" consists of a book with pictures of their birth family, photos of birthday parties, maybe the outside of flat they lived in plus a very brief chronology of their moves and social service interventions. Phrases such as *"Mummy Jane could not look after you properly because she was ill"* fail to mention the three days without food, how you were locked in a cupboard or the police drug raid which

found you in the dark, terrified, covered in sores and your own excrement. It doesn't mention the two dogs, three drug dealers, four soiled mattresses or the empty fridge which were also found in the flat. A few photographs taken during that police raid would be invaluable.

Just imagine the sensory triggers associated with that one scene. How does that fit with the photo of a smiling birth mother blowing out the candles on a cake or the description of her being loving and kind but sometimes angry? These conflicting messages are found in many life story books. It's as if there are two different jigsaw puzzles. The dark, scary one held by the child in their body/mind while the other puzzle shows a sunny, warm scene; a snapshot of an apparently happy family life where "sometime adults were angry". Surely that description fits all families, *generally happy, but sometimes adults are angry or ill"*? How does a child integrate those two contradictory puzzles?

Life story work does not equal a book of photos with captions.

Good life story work is ongoing; it integrates the past with the present, the shiny fragments mixes with the dirty stuff to map out a hopeful future.

The contradiction between the child's experience and the fragmented, rose-tinted photos and descriptions is hugely confusing for the child. It fuels misconceptions, shame, guilt, an unrealistic image of birth family members and conflicting memories about their early life. Consequently, the expectations, dreams and hopes an adoptee will create about their birth family are rooted in half truths, deception, huge gaps and falsehoods. This chaos will remain, unless therapeutic work is conducted to complete a new jigsaw which most accurately represents the child's body/mind sensual memories and makes sense of their history. The new jigsaw incorporates the warm, sunny pieces and the dark, scary chunks.

"Facts can be presented either in a way that helps the child understand and accept the past while raising self-esteem, or in a way that lowers feelings of self-worth. With experience, adults helping the child can learn to reframe even negative life experiences as positive strivings that went astray."
Vera Fahlberg, A Child's Journey Through Placement

Vera Falberg's wisdom has been present in the adoption and fostering world on both sides of the Atlantic for over two decades. Some professionals have absorbed her principles and practices, regrettably others have not. Her views on life story work are robust.

"Our past history confirms who we are and provides us with a sense of identity."
Vera Fahlberg, A Child's Journey Through Placement

Really good life story work enables the child to form a 'coherent narrative', a robust account of his past which he comprehends, fits with his sensory experiences and demonstrates it was not his fault. The child has to feel safe when hearing, reviewing and processing specific events and associated feelings. His own earlier perceptions and beliefs will modify, facilitating healing and the formation of a coherent narrative.

Magical thinking and fragmented self

Many children believe they were at fault and caused the horrors inflicted on them. One maltreated child believed she was a bad baby because she didn't change her own nappy. This perception stems from how a child thinks and their brain development. Between the ages of about eighteen months to seven years, a child personalises everything and believes their own thoughts, wishes or actions are responsible for what happens to them. This is known as "magical thinking". Claudia Jewett in Helping Children Cope with Separation and Loss, offers this example *"an adopted child told 'your parents couldn't take care of you' may understand this as 'there was something so bad or unlovable about ME that even my own parents couldn't manage or tolerate it'." She suggests this can be avoided by changing the phrase to "your parents couldn't look after ANY child at that time".*

A brilliant example of how language can reframe thinking and transform beliefs.

For many adopted children their knowledge about their lives prior to adoption is scant. Even if the records passed onto the adoptive parents are as accurate and detailed as possible; much is lost, unwitnessed and unknown. Hence the child often has a very confusing and contradictory image of himself and his history. Metaphorically his jigsaw and inner working model may only contain bits of blue, purple and red, hence the fragmented sense of self. The yellow, orange, green, black and white shades are missing. How does he fill these bits? With fantasy or hard truths?

> *"A major aspect of direct work is listening for the child's perceptions. Until we do this, we won't know if we are to expand their information or correct their misperceptions."*
> Vera Fahlberg, "A Child's Journey Through Placement"

Put simply, therapeutic work with the child has to start with the child's current beliefs, their understanding of the past and why they were removed and then adopted or fostered. The misconceptions generated by magical thinking need drastic modification. As the next chapter on reframing demonstrates, fresh perspectives when revisiting old memories can transform limiting beliefs into empowering beliefs and release embedded shame.

When and how should the truth be told?

There is a common misconception that children should not undertake therapy until they have been in an adoptive or foster placement for some time and have 'settled', or "when they are old enough to understand". This ignores the fact that the child's behaviour is driven by his beliefs about himself and the world. Until his sense of self has become less fragmented, his jigsaw pieces built into a comprehensible picture, and his internal working model more positive, his behaviour will reflect his internal conflict and chaos. The longer he is in this negative state the less time for brain rewiring and filling in the developmental gaps. It's the equivalent of removing a wounded soldier from the battlefield, giving emergency first aid but not taking him to hospital for an assessment, wound cleansing and possible surgery. The soldier may not die, but infection could set in, internal bleeding go unnoticed and eventually he might lose a limb or important organs which prevent him from ever functioning 'normally'. Early intervention makes sense, on so many levels and in so many situations.

For traumatised children the interventions need to be appropriate for their developmental age and functioning ability. The use of drama, drawing, modelling, music, play and metaphor is known to be effective, powerful and fits the trauma therapy criteria. Also because children can process more of the detail as they mature, therapy should be seen as an ongoing process which families dip into when necessary throughout childhood and probably into early adulthood.

The ground work and three-hundred-and-fifty-piece jigsaw should be done before adolescence, because puberty brings raging hormones, emotional extremes and an identity crisis. Remember parts of the brain go 'offline' causing teenagers to sometimes misinterpret the actions of others, hence adolescence is often a difficult time for many 'normal' families. For adoptive families it's frequently when things really explode, partly because of the unprocessed trauma, partly the shame and partly because the teenage adoptee's impulse control and self-regulation is poor. Now, thanks to Facebook, we can add the dynamite of unsupervised contact to that volatile mix.

What happens if a birth parent tells a teenager via Facebook that the neglect never happened? If that teenager has known the details for a number of years, seen the evidence and processed the consequences, he will have a very different perspective from the teenager who did not have the opportunity to process such events in a therapy and was just told by his adopters, "you were neglected."

Who facilitates the truth telling?

The release of shame, that all-pervading sense of personal worthlessness and badness, is a major component of effective therapeutic work. The journey from "I am bad" to "adults did bad things to me" is a bumpy one. It often requires the voicing of the unspeakable. Should those revelations come from the adoptive parents or from a neutral third party? My experience both personally and from speaking to other adopters and many professionals is no. No, it can't come from the adopters. Not because they can't or won't do it, but because the child will not listen to them or give them the same level of permission they offer a neutral third party, ideally, a specialist therapist.

Children who often have idealised their birth parents, feeling hurt or upset, will often say to their adoptive parents the equivalent of:

Δ "You don't know anything about them"

Δ "They loved me which is more than you do"

Δ "Don't you dare say that about her"

Δ "She would let me do..."

Δ "You would say that, because you are..."

Δ "What do you know you weren't there"

Δ "That's all lies, she loved me"

In essence: *"You do not have my permission to raise these issues about my birth parents and my past."*

A neutral third party is required. There are many reasons for this, including the child's shame. One eight-year-old who had already revealed some eye-watering memories told his mother, *"If I told you about that, you wouldn't like me anymore."*

Traumatised children need a safe place where the gruesome truth can be shared, along with the good stuff. The problem with much life story work is that the good stuff is documented, without fully referencing the shadow side. It is essential to provide good attachment based therapy addressing the darkness where the trauma lurks below the surface.

Although the adoptive parents don't take the lead in revealing and unpacking the past, they must be present and hear, see and participate in all the therapy. Excluding adopters suggests to the child that "the secrets" shared with the therapist are too awful for his adoptive parents to know. A great way to deepen shame. The child needs to see that his parents can hold that information, witness his pain and still love and nurture him. That is therapeutic. Also the fallout from sessions will be handled by the parents 24/7, so of course they need to have witnessed the process. Healing occurs both inside and outside therapy sessions.

For any reader who thinks that adopters can or should do this work unsupported , particularly in these times of financial constraint , I offer a few highly effective phrases I've heard therapists use in sessions which address a difficult piece of evidence from a child history or current challenging behaviour.

△ "We often find that children who were sexually abused know it happened to them. Did it happen to you?" (To a fifteen-year-old where file searching revealed the possibility.) The answer was "yes".

△ "Your birth mother asked you to decide whether you or your sister should be abused by her boyfriend. That must have been really hard for you."

△ "I think you are really hurting inside, and that's why sometimes you hit your mum, because in the past another mum hit and hurt you."

△ "Sometimes when children like you, who as babies were not fed for days, get very scared they steal food, money or things, because they feel empty inside."

△ "Another boy I worked with said he went rigid just before he got really angry and lost it. What do you notice before you explode?"

I don't think any adoptive or foster parent could deliver those words, even if they were a trained therapist, because, as a parent, your job is different. It is to support, listen, nurture and love that child, 24/7, despite their awful history and shame.

Another barrier is that adoptive parents are seldom allowed access to historical records and files, because it contains third-party information (data protection apparently). Hence technically only professionals can access the data. Fortunately some enlightened social workers and therapists share the data with adopters, but most are kept in the dark, just like mushrooms.

This is a ridiculous situation. There should be full disclosure of the child's case history to adopters before the child is placed for adoption.

Financial and political truths
Even though parents don't have the professional expertise and knowledge of attachment and trauma-trained therapists, they are, in the most part, expected to raise traumatised children without support or therapeutic input from professionals.

Apparently it's too expensive. Budgets are tight, don't you know.

BUBBLE WRAPPED CHILDREN

Clause 4 of the Adoption and Children Act 2002 states adopters are entitled to an assessment for adoption support, however the local authority *"must then decide whether to provide any such service to that person"*. So an adopted child is entitled to an assessment but whether the recommendations are implemented depends on the decision of the local authority, not the needs of the adoptive family.

This is not the place to argue the financial and political case or offer the cost benefit analysis; however the issue needs flagging so readers are under no illusions about the reality of adoption support, or lack of it. Promises are made and frequently broken. Prospective adopters beware. Get every promise in writing, because even though you trust the person delivering the message, staff transfer, organisations restructure, ministers get promoted and influencers change.

Until politicians and decision makers truly understand and acknowledge the consequences and long-term effect of childhood maltreatment, little will change for traumatized children, and the parents who live with them.

CHAPTER THIRTEEN

REFRAMING, TRANSFORMATION AND SABOTAGE

"With experience adults helping the child can learn to reframe even negative life experiences as positive strivings that went astray".
Vera Fahlberg, A Child's Journey Through Placement

One of the huge benefits of knowing the truth about our past is that it gives us a chance to re-examine our internal memories, update our inner working model and view of the world. A new interpretation of an old event can transform our perceptions and beliefs.

For 'normal' families the reservoir of historical knowledge is held by parents, grandparents, uncles, siblings and family friends who can tell stories about past events, celebrations, holidays, disasters and triumphs. Each person may have a slightly different perspective, but the narratives and photos will give a child a fairly consistent story. The phrase 'remember when' will trigger anecdotes at family events and anniversaries, so as the child matures his knowledge and understanding of himself and his family will be updated and events reframed. It's as if his personal database is being updated.

For an adopted child this is different. There is no method to update their old database because they don't have contact with the birth family who may also be unreliable witnesses. For an adopted child generally the only route to updating his database is to reframe events using historical written data and some intuitive guesswork.

One event, sensory perspectives
Chapter 1 included the 'rescue' of baby Tim by social workers and the police. Knowing the body keeps score, let's re-examine that particular scenario and incorporate learnings from previous chapters.

As a neglected, hungry child lying in a cot, Tim formed implicit memories based on that night's sensory experiences. The Trauma Criteria of overwhelming emotion or believing you might die, apply to Tim's experience.
In later years, Tim would have no way of expressing this overwhelming and traumatising experience verbally. He would not know that the smell of sour milk, Calvin Klein aftershave or stale urine was an olfactory sensory trigger which caused

in him to physical stiffen, be gripped with fear and his heart to pound. Those smells might not appear frequently, but what if Tim has a teacher who wears that aftershave? Tim might behave badly or dissociate in that teacher's class. No one would guess the underlying reason.

One event reframed

What if Tim aged ten had the opportunity in therapy to re-examine that event with independent evidence, the ongoing support of therapists and his adoptive parents?

Tim could draw pictures and talk about them. The scene could be rerun as an imaginary video or it could be re-enacted by therapists watched by Tim, who could then see what "baby Tim" needed; what his birth parents were doing, the role of the police, social workers and neighbours.

In the reframed scenario, ten-year-old Tim could see that he was helpless as a baby, he needed protecting. He was not bad, not worthless. Actually he was so important and special that others stepped in to protect him when his birth family couldn't. The flashing blue lights which scared him then was actually the signal that help had arrived. So the intention behind the noisy forced entry by the police was to rescue him. His parents fought the police partly because they were drunk and partly because they loved him and didn't want to lose him.

If Tim can reframe the event and see it as a positively intentioned action he has a fresh way of viewing the experience. He can start to shift from "I am bad" (because I generated disgust in the policeman) to worth protecting and therefore important i.e. "I am special". That is change at a core, identity level.

He can see that although his birth parents put up a fight to keep him, they were incapable of nurturing or parenting him or his siblings properly. It was not his fault. As a ten-year-old he can learn so much by looking at this event with fresh mature eyes. He can update his beliefs and personal database.

However this belief change work could not happen unless Tim had a safe place to learn these facts, process the data, face up to the harsh truths and their meaning. Tim may be sad, angry and hurt that his birth parents could not care for him. He may want to know his sisters are okay or why his parents drank so much. He may need to sob, rant or physically release the pent up rage. He may need to write (not send) a letter to his birth parents telling them how angry he is with them, or maybe loudly vocalise those sentiments directly towards a picture or physical model of them. All these are possible therapeutic strategies for the ten-year-old Tim. Again, expecting adopters or foster parents to do this unaided is preposterous.

Part of an ongoing process

If that particular event reframing is part of ongoing therapeutic work for Tim then over time his self-worth will increase, he will change some negative beliefs to more empowered thoughts and value himself more. Sadly because there will have been other ugly scenes resulting in a damaged self image, the process to remove the bubble wrap may take years. It requires consistent gentle unpacking of the issues in therapy plus much therapeutic reparenting for deep lasting transformation. Rather like changing the direction of an ocean-going liner, small adjustments early on yield better results than desperate wheel turning later, particularly when you're heading into rough waters.

Those rough waters come during adolescence when identity becomes a big issue, when brain rewiring occurs and children naturally gravitate away from the family they live with. As we will see later in this chapter, intrusions by birth family members via social networking can change teenage rough waters into a tsunami.

Outcomes from the reframing process

The truth is the catalyst for change; however it has to be processed and progressed at a rate suitable for the child. Like any long journey some parts are travelled quickly and smoothly, while other parts are slow, sticky, obstacle ridden scrabbles. Any reader who has participated in any form of self development, therapy or personal change work will know that processing is required before integration and behavioural change occurs. By moving through the learning cycle, you reflect, theorise, work out what it all means and sit with the emotions generated. Maybe you grieve for lost dreams and recognise you can only change yourself, not others. For adopted children acknowledging that their birth parents did the best they could; but it was deeply inadequate, sometimes cruel, often selfish with zero empathy, is hugely empowering; because it puts the responsibility where it truly lies; with the adults who failed them. That shift in mindset and parts integration does not happen without evidence, proof, much processing and support.

The chart below offers some examples of how the painful limiting beliefs formed by a traumatised child, listed in chapter one could transform into more empowering and positive beliefs. Remember most adopted children and many foster children will have experienced multiple forms of maltreatment.

Classification of infancy maltreatment	Possible impact & beliefs formed in infancy	Outcome from reframing events and samples of possible transformed beliefs
Emotional Abuse	*I am wrong, worthless, bad.* *They want me dead. should not be alive, I'm not wanted. I am unlovable*	When I was younger some adults called me names and hurt me, because they angry or on drugs. They were wrong. I am not ugly, stupid or bad. All children should be treated kindly and nurtured. I now have adults who love me and care about me. Some adults are kind others are not. I deserve consideration and happiness. I am lovable.
Physical Abuse	The world is a dangerous place, *I am bad & powerless.*	The world has both safe and dangerous places. I can keep myself safe. I can ask for help or protection when I need it from trustworthy people. I will not hurt myself or others.
Sexual Abuse	Destroyed innocence. *I can't trust anyone*	I am careful who I trust. I let people into my life, physical and emotional space at a pace of my own choosing.
Neglect	No self concept. *People abandon and reject me. I don't matter, life is hopeless, I am helpless &/or rage filled. Do I even exist?*	I am important, I have hope. I am powerful in my own life and can choose how I behave. When I feel empty I seek loving support from people I trust. I am satisfied with my life
Chaotic environment	No safe or secure base. *I am terrified.*	I put structure into my life. I can organise myself and my things. That helps me feel safe and in control. I am important.
Trauma	*I am going to die. I must disappear*	I am a survivor. I am resilient. I choose life and love. It is safe for me to be seen.

Just pause for a moment and think about the sort of behaviour you would expect to see from an eleven-year-old child whose beliefs and negative self-image had not changed since a traumatic infancy (i.e. the middle column). Now consider the behaviour of an eleven-year-old whose belief system and mindset been transformed into the more empowering beliefs and a positive internal working model (i.e. right-hand column).

Now fast forward two, three or four years and imagine the effect on those two children of raging hormones, a search for identity and the rational brain sometimes being 'offline. They are now teenagers. Which one would you prefer to live with?

Disclosure work

Many adopters have children who unconsciously recreate their birth family home in their bedrooms – hoarded half-eaten food, clothes, toys, hair gels, computer bits, urine soaked underwear, books etc, either hidden or all sprayed around the room often within minutes of it being 'tidied'. These kids are unconsciously recreating the chaos of their birth family, because it feels comfortable and familiar.

In one case the content of Social Services files were shared with an adoptive family during therapy. It detailed the chaotic environment; the rubbish bags in bedrooms, the dog shit and dirty nappies on the floor, the vomit-covered mattresses. This had a profound impact on fourteen-year-old Sonia, one of the teenagers. She started clearing and cleaning her room. She put tops back on bottles. She took dirty clothes, in a basket, to the kitchen for her Mother to wash. That was the impact of "disclosure work". Sonia was able to use her explicit memory to build the early events into a more useful and more accurate view of her past. It gave her a fresh perspective, new beliefs and transformed her behaviour.

An older sibling also participated in the disclosure work and therapy, however her bedroom remained chaotic. Seventeen-year-old Flora simply did not make the bed; she slept on top of the mattress, the duvet cover under a pile of clothes, the pillows bereft of cases. The family cat frequently scavenged in the room for chicken bones left over from a late night fast food binges. The carpet invisible beneath clothes, shoes, books, shopping bags, make up, toiletries, magazines and sweet wrappers. The adoptive mother had given up attempting to 'tidy' the room. Occasionally she would enter with black bags and clear the rotting food, but generally just closed the door. However Flora started making more effort at college and she now acknowledged her birth mother was an alcoholic, something she refused to countenance earlier. Flora was also becoming more aware of her own substance abuse.

The contrast between Sonia and Flora is a good example of how the same information will be interpreted, processed and utilised differently by traumatised children. It also demonstrates the need for therapeutic reparenting, ongoing support and therapy. Both the girls had been sexually abused. Maybe at an unconscious level Flora's unkempt bed helped her feel safe. Bed wetting is sometimes a feature of sexually abused children, because unconsciously they sense that a urine-soaked bed is less inviting to a potential abuser.

Literal reframing: take photographs.

Today we all carry mobile phones. One picture is worth a thousand words. That's why we should take photographs to record the full spectrum of a child's life: the sad and tragic incidents, the humdrum, everyday events plus the happy occasions. In Tim's scenario, the police and social services could have clicked and snapped away, then filed the photos for future use by the children and/or court proceedings. These would be priceless when integrated into life story work and therapy, making sense of his history. Such clear, unequivocal, visual evidence of the chaos he inhabited would empower Tim by portraying his life, confirming his sensory memories and help him to process and assimilate those sensory experiences into his present and future life. His trauma would be dissipated.

Photographs don't lie.

Yes, you could argue they can be doctored, touched up and amended. However we are not talking tabloid journalism here. These are photographs or videos taken by social workers, police officers and 'officials' as evidence, which are probably more reliable and detailed than a subjective account written by a professional because photographs contain masses of information. Photos also are neutral and honest offering interpretation by the viewer. Therefore they are more trustworthy than the accounts of individuals present.

Birth parents confronted with photographs evidencing the squalor in which they lived, cannot, months or years later, argue with them. It is solid, objective evidence. It refutes any claim that *"the place was just a bit untidy"*.

Sabotage

Let's consider Tim again and imagine he reconnects to one of his birth parents in his mid-teens.

What happens if:

1. His birth parent acknowledges the event; the hurt caused to Tim and says sorry?
2. His birth parent denies the event happened?
3. His birth parent denies the event happened and insists Tim is lying?
4. His birth parent denies the event and asserts "if you don't say it's a lie, I won't see you again"?
5. The birth parent says it was all Tim's fault?

Scenarios two, three, four and five confuse and hurt the child, but are happening through Facebook.

Scenario one does happen with facilitated contact, but not when connecting on Facebook.

How will Tim handle reconnecting to members of his birth family?

If Tim has three-hundred-and-fifty pieces of the jigsaw in position, what outcomes might there be?

If Tim has never had the opportunity to process this event or others from his early life, how will the reconnection affect him?

What will the reconnection with his birth family do to his relationship with his adoptive parents?

Who or what can Tim trust?

What criteria will Tim use to establish "the truth" about his past?

BUBBLE WRAPPED CHILDREN

CHAPTER FOURTEEN

PRINCIPLES OF CONTACT

"It would be sensible to conclude that contact can be a good thing only if the importance of truth is taken seriously and bad when truth is denied".
Lorne Loxterkamp

Contact contradictions

Contact probably generates more discussion and contradiction that any other subject in the adoption and fostering world. Partly because there is contradictory evidence on the benefits and usefulness of contact, partly because 'contact' can take many forms, and partly because of the beliefs of those making contact recommendations and implementing the plans.

Contact ≠ reunion

The concept of 'contact' is also contaminated by the past. The reunification of babies 'relinquished' by their birth mothers before the 1970s is a source of much media attention and speculation and generally considered to be a 'good thing'. We need to remember that these women were often forced to 'give up' their babies due to societal or family pressure linked to the stigma of illegitimacy.

Even though today, within the UK, 'illegitimacy' is not a reason for adoption, society has not quite grasped that difference and people still presume that mothers 'give up' their children for adoption. Their rose-tinted glasses mask ignorance and denial about child maltreatment. Society can't see the link between the abuse suffered by Baby Peter and children being removed and adopted. Sadly audiences of professionals and parents nod in agreement whenever I say *"children adopted today are frequently the Baby Peters who don't die".*

Acknowledging that ghastly reality puts a very different frame on the purpose, benefits and challenges of contact between children, and the adults who maltreated them. In Trauma Attachment and Family Permanence 2003 Alan Burnell, a cofounder of Family Futures states:

"In the majority of contemporary adoption situations, direct contact represents contamination and retraumatisation, unlike baby adoptions where contact represents continuity and the building blocks of future identity. Unless some degree of reparation is facilitated this relationship pathology continues as part of the child's inner representations, distorting his self-perceptions and current interactions."

BUBBLE WRAPPED CHILDREN

The question "Is contact good for children?" has no easy answer for professionals, parents or researchers. When Jeanette Cossar spoke at a BAAF conference in February 2011, she agreed with her colleagues David Howe and Elspeth Neil, from the University of East Anglia, stating: *"There are no straightforward answers to the broad questions about whether or not contact will benefit specific children. Contact can be a resource or protective factor, but it can also be a risk."*

Evidence-based research v anecdotal evidence

There are differing and conflicting views in the adoption world about the benefits of contact after a child has been placed with his adoptive family. There are contradictory pieces of research from both the USA and UK and unfortunately sometimes blanket conclusions are drawn from single, well publicised studies.

During my membership of an adoption panel, one social worker recommended quarterly, face-to-face contact between a four-year-old, who had been in foster care for two years, and her violent birth mother. When panel members challenged the contact plan, the social worker replied, "Research shows contact is important for the child's identity." A naïve response, because even if that's the finding of one piece of research, would it be at the cost of retraumatize the child every few months? The child's identity issues could be tackled from a different direction. Panel were told the contact plan would change to indirect letterbox contact. I hope it did.

Many of the studies about contact are based on a very small sample group. The studies involve birth parents who will, for years, cooperate with both the contact arrangements and the researchers. This is actually a very small subset of birth families, yet as the anecdote in the previous paragraph demonstrates, some professionals will make big generalisations from these findings.

In the recent book "Supporting Direct Contact after Adoption", published by BAAF in 2011, Neil Cossar et al report findings which were based on interviews with:
- Δ   Thirty-nine birth relatives spanning three generations of which twenty-one were birth parents
- Δ   Fifty-one adoptive parents
- Δ   Four long-term foster carers.

Their finding included:

- Δ *"Adoptive parents, adopted children and birth relatives varied widely in terms of their strengths and risks, suggesting that contact is likely to be more complex in some cases than in others".*
- Δ *Many children were still struggling with the impact of their early history*
    - ▲ *44% had emotional or behavioural difficulties*
    - ▲ *51% were reported to have very complicated feelings about their birth parents and status as an adopted person*
    - ▲ *29% had problems in their relationship with their adoptive parents*

I don't dispute these findings, or other good adoption research conducted by the University of East Anglia or other academic bodies. My concern is that these small studies seem to carry so much more weight than buckets of anecdotal evidence from adopters and foster carers.

In December 2010 when speaking at a BAAF conference in Cardiff, I asked the seventy-five participants (social workers and other adoption and fostering professionals) what percentage of birth parent they thought cooperated and collaborated with social services and contact arrangements. To my surprise, the vast majority suggested it was less than two percent. Of course this is not tested data; it's just an indicator, a straw poll, and hearsay. However, with the level of expertise and experience in the room, it felt significant to those of us present.

Yes, post adoption, a small number of birth parents will fully collaborate with professionals, will be able to put the child's needs first, behave responsibly and create a positive and useful experience for the child. Fantastic.

But, from the birth parent perspective this is a big ask. This birth mother may have limited emotional intelligence and executive functioning skills, may have mental health issues or unresolved trauma and is grieving for the loss of her child(ren). You are asking that woman to put her own feelings aside and concentrate on the needs of the child. Oh, and you are probably expecting her to do it without any ongoing support. Dream on. It's unrealistic and cruel.

Is it any wonder that research into post-adoption contact has such a small number of participants? Despite the tiny sample sizes the findings are broadcast widely and frequently mapped across to numerous other care planning cases.

The other major players in post-adoption contact are the adoptive parents and child(ren). It is a big ask for them too. All participants would probably want to know the purpose, possible benefits and potential hazards plus the form contact would take. What will actually happen?

Types of contact in adoption and fostering

1 **DIRECT CONTACT** *SUPERVISED* △ Standard Face to Face △ Facilitated Face to Face	2 **DIRECT CONTACT** *UNSUPERVISED* Any unsupervised moments Texts Phone calls Emails Social Networking sites
4 **INDIRECT CONTACT** *SUPERVISED* △ Letterbox – letters △ Letterbox – photos △ Letterbox – gifts	3 **INDIRECT CONTACT** *UNSUPERVISED* △ Facebook Stalking △ Getting information from a third party △ Physically Lurking

While in foster care, contact for a child tends to be in Quadrant 1, direct, with a mixture of supervised and unsupervised meetings. Post adoption the contact tends to be Quadrant 4, indirect, supervised contact. Some adoptive placements have direct contact with family members, but generally it is the low key, letterbox contact, which may be one or two-way. Once or twice a year adopters send letters and photographs to the birth family via a neutral third party, probably the local authority. Birth family may send information via the letterbox system; the content is vetted and forwarded to the adoptive family if appropriate. Sometimes the communication from the birth family to the child talks about reunification, how the parent is actively looking for the child or is critical of the adoptive family. These letters are not passed on, but kept on file.

Purposes of post-adoption contact

The purpose of contact is simply to help a child have a better sense of themselves and their past. To help with identity issues, loss, grief, confusion, the sense of rejection, answer genetic and biological inheritance queries, stop people being 'frozen in time' and to prevent later shocks.

Put simply, the purpose of post adoption contact is to help the child. But to help the child how? Help the child with what? Suggestions include:

Δ it's to give the child reassurance that their birth family are okay
Δ help the child with identity issues
Δ see evidence of biological and genetic inheritance
Δ stops the child feeling they were rejected by the birth family
Δ prevents shocks in later life
Δ diminishes the longing children feel for their birth family
Δ shows the child their birth family still love, value and care for them
Δ that to have a positive feelings and view of themselves, children must have a positive view of their birth parents

After many years' experience working with adoptive families who have contact, the consultant child and adolescent psychotherapist Lorne Loxterkamp has changed his view on the benefits of contact. In his article "Contact and Truth: The unfolding Predicament in Adoption and Fostering" he suggests that when, in an effort to create positive feelings about the birth family there is concealment, falsification and lies about the child's history, it is damaging to the child. *"The firmly held belief that the effects of harm can be reduced by promoting a positive view of the character of the abusive or neglectful birth parent is ill-founded and serves another kind of harm."*

If just a positive image of the birth family is promoted a child may think:

Δ My birth family are okay now, so why can't I live with them?
Δ They love me, so why can't I live with them?
Δ I was to blame
Δ They are good, so I must be bad

Contact works for the child when birth parents:

Δ Take responsibility and offer a coherent account of what life was like for the child when living with them
Δ Say Sorry, it was our fault, not yours.
Δ Give blessing to where the child is currently living.

Expecting birth parents to fulfil these three criteria without preparatory work and supported is unreasonable.

To put it bluntly; contact handled badly can retraumatize a child and damage the relationship between the adopters and the child. Good contact must have purpose and meaning for all participants. That doesn't just happen because a few people are all in the same room. Supervised contact is not facilitated contact. That distinction is important. Supervised contact generally has a preventative frame, to stop any harm right now, not to undo the damage from the past. It is reactive. The logistics may be organised beforehand, but the content is not pre-planned. Facilitated contact is proactive, has a pre-planned before, during and after. The section below gives a flavour of the process.

One example of an effective facilitated contact

Eight years after placement and as a component of a therapy plan, my children each had contact sessions with members of their birth family. These were facilitated by Family Futures, an adoption support agency. For months before, during and after the contact session, each participant – the birth parents, adoptive parent and child – had their own specific therapist to support and aid them.

The entire process took months to set up and was planned like a military operation. Two rooms were booked in a neutral venue, so people didn't accidentally bump into each other. The second room offered privacy, a "decompression chamber" if necessary. Within the main 'contact room', seating had been pre-planned, the chairs placed in a wide circle with each therapist sitting next to the person they were supporting. Low coffee tables at the sides held tissues and water, so no physical barriers, but with enough personal space between the players to feel unthreatened. The individual entry and exits were orchestrated; the last in and first out were myself and the child. The psycho-geography of the room well thought through and it felt 'safe'.

Questions were pre-planned, written and circulated to all, so all parties were able to consider and compose their answered before the meetings and there would be no surprises. Some particularly difficult and painful questions were voiced or answered by the therapist, when it was too difficult for the child or birth parent.

Each contact session between the individual child and specific birth family member was held on a separate day. The contact day itself was really tough; for the child, the birth parent and me. Quite high stress for the facilitators too. The day involved an early start, late finish, lengthy train journeys, taxis, a secure venue, close monitoring of the area in case uninvited birth family members turned up, plus the anxiety that the birth parent might be intoxicated, postpone or simply fail to appear. The potential for disappointment was enormous.

However the outcome was worthwhile. The birth parent was able to take some responsibility for the past, gave blessing to the adoptive placement and a large dose of reality destroyed some fantasies for everyone. Contact affected each child differently. It had some positive effects on family life. The birth parent was delighted to see the children. Without high quality facilitation, this contact could not and would not have happened.

Based on my personal experience and other people's stories, I think it is impossible for any birth parent to fulfil those three requirements without considerable external support. Facilitation is essential. Birth parents, adopted children and adopters need support if contact is to have a useful, coherent outcome.

There is a footnote to this story. One birth parent emailed the (over eighteen) children via Facebook about seven years later. There was considerable fallout and ongoing consequences.

Requirements of facilitated contact

Readers who want to understand the complexities of facilitated contact would benefit from reading "Contact as Therapy" by Alan Burnell, Chapter 11 in Trauma, Attachment and Family Permanence edited by Caroline Archer. The list below is my high level overview and is simply intended to provoke thought; it is not an exhaustive list.

- Δ   First do no harm
- Δ   Prepare, prepare, plan, prepare
- Δ   No surprises
- Δ   Ensure safety: physical, psychological, emotional
- Δ   Involve the child, adopters, birth family throughout
- Δ   Step into the shoes of each player and see their perspective, fears, hopes
- Δ   Prearrange and agree questions especially the difficult ones.
- Δ   Clarify and manage everyone's expectations,
- Δ   Provide solid, appropriate support for each player before, during and after
- Δ   Ensure each player is in a 'good state' on the day.

Participants need to be very clear on expectations, intentions and outcomes. This is very different to the direct contact which normally occurs when children are being fostered. It also differs from much post adoption contact currently because the "truth telling" is absent. What if, you reframe the purpose of contact into an opportunity to:

- Δ   heal trauma
- Δ   make sense of sensory triggers
- Δ   acknowledge the child's implicit memories

Δ provide evidence to change the child's deeply held negative beliefs
Δ truth tell
Δ acknowledge the pain experienced
Δ allow the opportunity for birth parents to see that their children accept them and their deeds

Questions or statements might include:
Δ Did you know that someone pushed things inside me and hurt me?
Δ Because you broke my arm and didn't take me to hospital, it healed crookedly. I sometimes find it difficult to write because it hurts.
Δ Why didn't you stop Daddy hitting me?
Δ I am scared of the dark and still have night terrors
Δ Why did you spend money on drugs when I was hungry and needed food?
Δ Did you want me?
Δ I'm fourteen, have never consented to sex, but tested positive for an STD when I was nine. How come?
Δ I am sad you could not look me and want you to know I am happy and hope you are too
Δ I want you to know I love both you and my adoptive parents

There are thousands more possible questions. Each child and situation will be different. To expect birth parents to answer these types of questions without support is cruel and unrealistic. However children need these painful questions answered to integrate the knowledge and piece together their own complex jigsaw puzzle.

Contact via Facebook offers none of the criteria for good contact
None of the questions above will be asked or answered via social networking sites. Contact via social networking offers none of the emotional security, honesty or physical protection implicit in facilitated contact. But it is so easy; so very, very easy to set up and:
Δ Offers great expectations
Δ Provides no emotional support to anyone
Δ Can be conducted secretly
Δ Has safeguards
Δ Allow all parties to lie and distort without accountability or offering evidence
Δ Puts vulnerable adults and children at risk
Δ Ignores the painful past
Δ Makes retraumatisation likely

Contact via social networking is such a new phenomenon that, as yet, we have no endings to the individual stories or collective patterns. What we can discern is the trajectory of individual children's lives being rerouted. We can't yet step back to take the long view, only witness current events and make educated guesses and predictions. By the 2020s we will have some answers, patterns, conclusions, specific and general data. For now we must watch the children currently battling with adolescence and reconnection with their birth families with crossed fingers. Yes of course they would benefit from good adoption support, therapy and facilitated contact right now, but… money is tight don't you know!

Vaccinate against dis-ease

We do have the opportunity to prepare the next wave of children from social networking intrusions: those who are not yet fully into adolescence, those under eleven and those not yet born. These children can construct their nine or fifteen-piece jigsaw when they are at infant school, then in junior school tackle the seventy, one-hundred-and-eighty and three-hundred-and-fifty-piece versions. During Secondary School five hundred and seven-hundred-and-fifty-piece versions can be explored, with the full thousand-piece tackled as an adult. Obviously the construction of each jigsaw needs input and support from suitable therapists, and except for the thousand-piece, adoptive parents must be included in the sessions. Sometimes facilitated contact with members of the birth family will be desirable.

Medically vaccinations are given to children so they develop an adaptive immunity to a specific disease. A tiny dose of the disease administered by the vaccine stimulates the child's immune system which responds by developing a protective resistance to that disease. So exposure to that disease in later life has no or minimal effect. We must vaccinate in preparation for Facebook intrusions, lies, false expectations, distortions and fantasy.

This is not a vaccine against the birth family; it is against the future dis-ease a child may experience. I use the hyphen quite deliberately. The lack of 'ease', the fragmented self, the shame and the shadow cause the problems; while truth and understanding bring relief, healing and self acceptance. As the next chapter demonstrates, adolescence is tough for any child; an adopted or fostered child wracked with fear, guilt, knowledge gaps and anger is a ticking time bomb.

"Experience is not what happens to a man:
it is what a man does with what happens to him."
Aldous Huxley

CHAPTER FIFTEEN

ADOLESCENCE: IT'S A QUESTION OF IDENTITY

"Anna Freud said essentially that adolescence was redoing childhood in a different way. Others have said that teenagers are really two-year-olds with hormones and wheels."
Holly Van Gulden, Real Parents, Real Children

Door slamming, shouting, sulking, weeping and rebelling are typical observable behaviours in teenagers. Adolescence is a tricky period. It's a time of shifting identity, re-evaluation of values and because friends and peers become more important, necessitates some disconnection from the family. For an adopted child there are even more layers of confusion to be added to that complex, emotionally charged process. Which family do they disconnect from? Whose values do they identify with?

"The primary psychological tasks of adolescence echo the tasks of years one to five. The young person must once again psychologically separate, this time from the family, finding their place in society as a whole rather than solely as a member of the family. He or she is cutting emotional ties instead of seeking gratification within the family. A surge of identity formation once again accompanies the separation process." Vera Falberg: A Child's Journey Through Placement.

What if years one to five were filled with chaos, confusion, trauma and poor attachments?

We all know that any structure built on weak foundations will sink or collapse if too much weight is put on it. Returning to the metaphoric wall of developmental needs metaphor, introduced in Chapter 2; adolescence exerts a heavy weight the wall. If the wall is the spring board to adulthood, then the weak foundations, crumbling bricks and gaps in maltreated children's walls will cause lost footings, accidents and big crashes as these children attempt to leap into adulthood.

Before social networking, adolescence was an opportunity to rewire the adoptee's teenage brain by continuing therapeutic reparenting. Remembering that 15% of the brain is 'rewired' during adolescence, this was an opportunity to fill and repair some gaps in the wall, to teach emotional regulation, build a stronger sense of self and offer stability at home, within the adoptive family. Because of unsupervised contact via Facebook during adolescence this healing opportunity is currently being jeopardised or lost.

Typical 'normal' adolescent development

Adolescence is the period of transition from childhood to adulthood. In the western world it takes years, and as living away from home is generally a criteria for being an adult, it can be argued adolescence is lengthening because financial constraints stop offspring leaving home. Adolescence takes individuals along a bumpy path from childhood dependence, obedience and no sexual interaction to adult independence, self-reliance, responsibility and meaningful sexual relationships. This path is bumpy for parents too.

Fahlberg and Van Gulden recognise two specific phases when identity formation is a central issue and generates many doubts and enquiries.

Δ   Early adolescence: when the process of psychologically separating from parents and identifying more with the peer group raises the questions:

▲ Who am I?

▲ Where do I belong?

Δ   Very late adolescence: when a considerable amount of independence has been established, raising the questions:

▲ What kind of person am I?

▲ What do I believe in?

▲ How do I relate to my parents and siblings now I don't live with them?

These exploratory questions will primarily be unconscious with the answer evidenced by the adolescent's behaviour, not their words.

Identity formation in adolescence requires two levels of separation:

1. External: emotional energy is drawn away from parents and refocused on peers
2. Internal: disengagement from identification with early childhood models (parents) while new diverse models (peers, teachers, heroes) are internalised

The adjoining chart, primarily based on Fahlberg's work, is self-explanatory and included so readers can see how unexpected reconnection with birth family members at specific ages can throw a child off their 'normal developmental path', particularly in relation to identity formation. Fahlberg states: *"In general, during adolescence young people experience a year of expanding horizons and new challenges, followed by a year of consolidation of gains. Both parents and teenagers can expect a year of turmoil followed by a year with some measure of reprieve in which to renew and once again strengthen relationships before moving into another year of rapid change."*

Age	Typical adolescent behaviour and attitudes	Possible Identity Questions
11	More angry than at 10. Always moving. Emotionally unstable, easily flies into a rage or giggling fits. Assertive, curious, investigative, talkative, sociable. Yells, slams doors, violent verbal retorts Tires easily, but doesn't want to go to bed. Begins to see Mum and Dad as separate individuals and is critical of them. Poorest time for relationships with siblings	Who am I? Where do I belong? What would my life be like in a different family?
12	More compliant, more reasonable than at 11. Tries to win approval of others. Peer group increasingly important. School can be a source of great satisfaction because of their new capacity for prolonged periods of factual learning and increased conceptual ability or the opposite for children who find school a challenging, hostile dysregulating environment.. Likeable, great enthusiasm, often assert themselves by talking back to their parents	Who am I? Where do I belong? What would my life be like in a different family? What groups want me?
13	Less outgoing and inquisitive. Isolated and moody. Withdrawal from family to reflect and incorporate experiences. Introspective. Gazing into mirrors to integrate body changes perception of self and self-assurance. Sensitive to criticism but critical of parents. Argumentative. Get annoyed, irritated, sulk, tears, angry tears. Physically withdraw, door slamming. School is source of gratification for good students.	Who am I? Where do I belong? What would my life be like in a different family? Why does everyone hate me?
14	Expansive and outgoing again. Less withdrawn. More objective, capable of self appraisal. Anger expressed under breath rather than out loud.	Who am I? Where do I belong?
15	Frequently appear lazy and indifferent. Similar to 13, preoccupied with feelings and thoughts. Resistance to even reasonable restrictions imposed by others. Growing self awareness and perceptiveness, resolving own limitations and potential.	Who am I? Where do I belong? What can I do? What can I become? Why is life so unfair?
16	More self assurance and self reliance. Emotions generally in control.	What can I do? What can I become? Where am I going? What will I do? How will I get there? What do I believe in?
17-adult	Less Oppositional. It's ok to be different from peers. Increased tolerance. Start looking towards independence and developing self care skills (physical and emotional)	What can I do? What can I become? How and when will I take control of my life? Where am I going? What will I do? How will I get there? What do I believe in?

BUBBLE WRAPPED CHILDREN

Holly Van Gulden in Real Parents Real Children splits her developmental phases into early (11-13/15), middle (15-17) and late 17-19/21ish) adolescence. Like Vera Fahlberg she makes the distinction that the physical onset of puberty does not coincide with the psychological traits associated with adolescence.

Early adolescence
  Δ   First attempts to establish a distinct identity
  Δ   Start emotional separation from family
  Δ   Practice being different from family and similar to peers (hair, clothes, music)
  Δ   Desire to belong to peer groups and be physically seen in public with peers
  Δ   Moody
  Δ   Easily embarrassed, especially by and with parents
  Δ   Common time for resurgence of grief for the loss of birth parents.

Middle adolescence
  Δ   Practice intimacy
  Δ   Consolidation of sense of self based on past, present and hopes for the future

Late adolescence and early adulthood should bring answers to most identity questions if a single coherent sense of self has developed. These may include:

Q.   Who am I?
A.   I have a sense of continuity and sameness, at my core my identity, values and beliefs remain the same in all groups and settings, although I may modify my behaviours
Q.   Where do I belong?
A.   There is a place for me in the world, within my family and my peers.
Q.   Where am I going, what will I do, and how will I get there?
A.   I have a sense of where my life is heading, the roles I currently hold and those I want in the future.
Q.   How and when will I take control of my life?
A.   I am leaving home in a planned and controlled manner, which is strengthening my self-image and self-esteem.

Some compare and contrast questions relating to parents may be asked repeatedly throughout adolescence.
  Δ   How am I the same as you?
  Δ   How am I different from you?
  Δ   What parts of you do I reject?
  Δ   Which parts of you do I admire and want to emulate?
  Δ   Which of your values do I hold and which do I drop?

134

At the same time an adolescent is looking at friends, peers, heroes, role models and considering:

Δ Who do I admire?
Δ Who do I want to imitate?
Δ What am I not going to be?
Δ To which groups do/don't I want to belong?
Δ Who and what do I think is wrong?
Δ Where, when and with whom do I feel most myself?
Δ Where, when and with whom do I feel most alienated?
Δ Who understands me?

These thoughts are sometime conscious, other times unconscious. They are signposts and junctions on the tumultuous journey from childhood to truly becoming an adult. The answers may change and modify at different stages of development and after specific events which shake and shape the identity formation. Being accepted or rejected by a specific group will affect the shape of your identity. Deciding you are sporty or cool or academic or ugly or musical or unpopular or rebellious or fat or nerdy or worthless or clever will form aspects of your identity and your resultant behaviour.

'Normal' adolescents gravitate away from their parents and family towards their peers. A simple, straight line movement: towards or away from.

Adopted adolescent children are pulled in three directions because they have two sets of parents and their peers. Obviously they will gravitate away from their adoptive parents and towards peers; but in what direction does the pull of their birth parents take them? How does this new dimension complicate their adolescence and identity formation?

This is where values come into play. Our values are the things we believe are important. Along with our beliefs they motivate us into action. If we honour our values we feel more congruent. If our values are violated we may feel offended, angry, hurt or upset. Something which mattered to us has been disregarded or ignored by another.

An adolescent will often reject some of his parent's values as he explores his own identity and his beliefs. He may choose the values of his peer group which are in conflict with his parents. An adopted adolescent has the extra complicating dimension. Which birth parent values does he identify with and which does he reject? What does he know about his birth parents' values? What does he know about his birth parents?

BUBBLE WRAPPED CHILDREN

Even if they were abandoned hours after birth, Holly Van Gulden says the three things every adopted child knows about their birth parents are:

1. they were irresponsible
2. they were fertile
3. they had sex

By contrast, their adoptive parents are incredibly responsible, infertile and never have sex. Oh come on, whatever your age, no one imagines their own parents having sex.

"I don't want to be like you, I want to be like them"

As adolescence is traditionally the time to disengage from the parents with whom you reside, why wouldn't the adopted children gravitate away from their adopters and towards their birth parents?

What if those birth parents appear to share similar values to the adolescent? What if these conflict with the values of the adoptive parents? Surely this will increase the teenager's attraction towards the birth parents and away from the adopters.

"I hate you Mum because you won't let me do x" is a common adolescent thought. For adopted children it can genuinely be followed by *"my real Mum would let me do x"*. The adopter's rules and boundaries are seen as overly strict with *"I don't want to be like you, I want to be like them"* the frequent unspoken, underlying belief.

For adopted adolescents the *"how am I the same as you and how am I different"*, question can be directed at both the adoptive and the birth parents.

The answers will be very different depending on how much truth the adolescent knows about his past. How much detail does he have? Reflect for a moment and consider how the chart below might be completed by an eleven/thirteen/fifteen-year-old with limited information (nine pieces) or substantial information (three-hundred-and-fifty pieces)?

View of Birth Parents with 9 pieces of jigsaw information	Questions	View of Birth Parents with 350 pieces of jigsaw information
	How Am I the same as you?	
	How am I different from you	
	What parts of you do I reject?	
	Which parts of you do I admire and want to emulate?	
	Which of your values do I hold and which do I drop?	

Gaps and the benefits of truth telling

Lorne Loxterkamp considers that *"the emotional turbulence of adolescence consists of the working out, and the testing out, of that which should be accepted as one's own and of that which should be rejected."* He argues that while part of our identity is formed from what we choose to hold on to and admire, *"there is an identity derived from dissociating oneself from that which is wrongheaded, objectionable, hateful, contemptible, reprehensible or simply alien. There is an identity derived from acceptance, but there is also identity derived from rejection, to form an identity is to accept this and reject that."*

He argues that *"being in possession of the detailed facts provides better grounds for determining the proper attitude towards birth family and therefore ones identity".*

For many adopted children there may be significant gaps in their knowledge. If they know little or even nothing about their birth father there is a huge space for fantasies and unanswered identity questions. *"I wonder if my father…"* Sometimes birth mothers choose not to reveal the name of the father, other times they don't know it. Either way, the adopted adolescent has a huge void to negotiate if 50% of their identity heritage is unknown.

The drama triangle played out during adolescence

"I hate you"; "you are so horrible to me"; you stop me doing what I want"; "it's all your fault". Frequent sentiments thought and sometimes vocalised by adolescents towards their parents. Classic 'victim' phrases, where the parents are fulfilling the role of perpetrator. The rescue figure might be a friend or peer group, while the teenager is the poor misunderstood victim.

In addition to nurturing, adoptive and foster parents offer structure, boundaries and rules for their children. Along with the vast majority of parents, they expect children to attend school, obey the normal rules of society, refrain from violence, stealing and dishonesty. To ensure their safety, parents want to know where a child is going and with whom. They expect adolescents to obey reasonable curfews, house rules and demonstrate some consideration for others. The application of those rules and holding the boundaries cause adolescents distress because part of their job description is to challenge the rules, however reasonable and appropriate they are.

Because of their early life experiences, adopted and fostered teenagers frequently hit the boundaries very hard and simply refuse to follow the rules. They may engage in high risk taking behaviour, staying out all night, abusing alcohol and drugs, having violent outbursts and demonstrating "challenging behaviour" (a phrase used in professional reports which I hate because it so diminishes the magnitude of the disruption, pain and terror experienced). This oppositional behaviour is a consequence of infant maltreatment. If a child's internal state is fear or terror, when hyper-aroused, their exhibited behaviour will be defiance and aggression. This is true for toddlers and adolescents. Holding and calming a child having a toddler tantrum is possible when they are physically small and the parent is physically stronger. Holding a teenager throwing a toddler tantrum is close to impossible and may result in parental bruises or broken bones.

Pity one adoptive parent who stood in front of the door, intent on preventing a thirteen-year-old girl leaving the house at 11pm, determined on meeting her twenty-one-year-old boyfriend for sex and drugs. That day her mother ended up with a broken window and two black eyes. The girl stormed out, perceiving herself as the victim, her adoptive mother as perpetrator and boyfriend as rescuer. The police did not see it that way. You might not either. Domestic violence inflicted by children on their adoptive parents is not a widely recognised phenomenon. Who is the victim; who the perpetrator?

For adopted and foster children, the rescuer could be perceived as the birth parent(s). The parents with whom they reside are the perpetrators; while the birth family can easily fulfil the role of rescuers inside the child's head. However now, thanks to Facebook, that fantasy can become a physical reality. Birth parents are "rescuing" their children from adopters.

Health warning
This chapter and the chart primarily outlined "typical" adolescent behaviours, so readers should bear in mind:
Δ the gaps in the "needs wall" of maltreated children
Δ adopted and fostered children will seldom follow the "normal" child development path
Δ children maltreated in infancy are likely to have significant delay in their emotional and psychological development which will be reflected in their behaviour and regression is common.

While reconnections with birth family via social networking can occur at any chronological age, the adopted child may be functioning at a much younger level emotional and psychological age, so the consequences are difficult to predict and manage. For example if a girl is chronologically fifteen, emotionally fluctuating between five and thirteen, with a reading age of eleven, numerical skills of nine, has symptoms of Developmental Trauma Disorder, is highly sexually active and abusing drugs and alcohol, the chart above is probably not an accurate reflection of her world.

Adolescent idealism

Another drama triangle perspective sometimes played out is linked to the idealism which is a common characteristic in late adolescence. This idealism might centre on the adolescent wanting to rescue birth family members. When those unrealistic goals are not met, adoptees may perceive themselves as unworthy failures, further denting their self-esteem.

Learning how to help others without either rescuing or controlling them is a task many adults fail to master. It takes considerable emotional maturity to appreciate that another person may not be willing or able to transform and sometimes, by fulfilling the "rescuer" role, you enable the other person to remain stuck in "victim mode". Sophisticated, dispassionate thinking, the ability to step back and not be sucked into the drama is a tall order for idealistic young adults.

This shows yet another reason for ongoing adoption support and therapeutic input which should continue until at least twenty-one.

BUBBLE WRAPPED CHILDREN

CHAPTER SIXTEEN

STILL SCREAMING, MORE BIRTH PARENT PERSPECTIVES

I have been very surprised at people's reaction when I've said that my children's birth mother contacted them unexpectedly by sending a message through Facebook.

Bizarrely, "Isn't that illegal?" is the most frequent comment from those not involved in the adoption world. After the 'OMG' reaction, adopters and social workers are more interested in the 'how', 'what happened next' and 'how have the kids responded' questions.

The fact that birth parents are attempting to reconnect with their children lost via adoption, should come as no surprise. They have always wanted to. Facebook, social networking and the internet simply make it possible quickly and quietly from the privacy and comfort of your own home.

Most birth parents have never stopped loving or thinking about their children. However I believe there is a distinction to be made between men and women.

Some birth fathers have no interest in the children they sire, others have a superficial interest, some have a concern, a few are 100% committed to their child and are deeply affected by the child's adoption.

For a birth mother it's different. She carried the child inside her for nine months. She bore the pain of the birth. Her body will always have reminders, physically emotionally and in her cellular memory. Throughout her life, there will always be sensory triggers and events reminding her, consciously or unconsciously that she unwillingly lost a child. Her grief is unresolved; her loss enormous; her pain still fresh, she is "still screaming".

Over the past few decades, the majority of research, practice and knowledge is based on birth mothers' experiences. Anecdotally, birth mothers and their side of the family seem to be reconnecting most, hence in this chapter I will specifically talk about birth mothers and look at possible vignettes in her life post adoption.

Motivation

Many birth mothers have an unrequited love and are stuck with the unresolved grief and loss that has probably magnified over the years of separation from their child. Their motivation for reconnecting is to reduce their pain, shame, guilt and hurt. Instead of the question "why do they send emails via Facebook", the more powerful question is "why wouldn't they".

The grief cycle explained in Chapter 7 is repeated here as a reminder that birth mothers may still be locked in pathological grief.

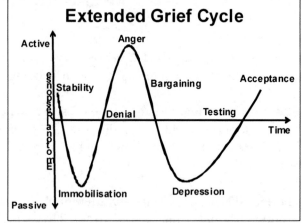

Herzberg motivation theory tells us man has two sets of needs; one set as an animal to avoid pain, and the second set as a human being to grow psychologically. Avoiding pain obviously takes priority. Reducing existing pain is a great motivator. Reducing pain is a behavioural driver for many birth parents and goes some way to explaining their actions over many years, which superficially may seem contradictory and self-defeating.

What sort of personal relationships does she have? With low self-worth and often a sense of hopelessness she is a prime target for an abusive relationship with a controlling man. She may act like a victim; he is powerful and rescues her. This may then shift to controlling and sometimes violent behaviour. The drama triangle is enacted. He shifts from rescuer to powerful perpetrator; she stays the wounded victim, confirming her sense of worthlessness and hopelessness.

The high stress levels birth mothers experience affects their health. Some display mental health problems, anxiety, depression, dreams about being reunited with their child, flashbacks about their removal. Some show the symptoms of Post Traumatic Stress Disorder.

There are always reminders of her loss. What does a birth mother do on her son's birthday? Celebrate? Remember? Mourn? Fantasise about what the child might be doing? Hallucinate on what she would do with him? How does she handle other anniversaries and festivities? Christmas is an obvious challenge.

What is her reaction to receiving information and photos if she has letterbox contact? How does she manage if it stops? Maybe the adopters stop sending data or she has moved, not left a forwarding address and not informed the agency facilitating the letterbox contact, so letters never reach her.

What if she has never received information about her children? Inside her head her son may be frozen in time, stuck at the age she last saw him, despite now being able to vote.

A birth mother seldom knows where her child has been placed, so birth mothers may always be on the lookout for their child, sometimes thinking she spots him. When child abductions or murders occur there can be great fear if the age and sex corresponds to her own child. Later relief, then guilt when newspaper photos establish that it's another family's misfortune.

How does she cope when for years or decades she hears nothing about her children? Her own personal jigsaw has gaping holes. How does a birth mother escape from these overwhelming feelings, the toxic shame, the guilt, the intrusive thoughts, the grief and deep pain? How does she exit the grief cycle?

Grief reduction strategies
What strategies might she employ? One way to escape is with drugs or alcohol. Another is to become numb. Maybe having more children will ease the pain. Focusing on something else might work, a crisis-filled life, an abusive relationship or a succession of them. Directing anger at others or turning it inwards and self-harming can offer temporary relief.

Another way of resolving this pain is to reconnect to her child and attempting to re-establish a relationship. At times the urge to reconnect with the child forcibly removed from her must be utterly overwhelming.

Before Facebook it took time and considerable effort to reconnect. Tracing occurred via the National Adoption Register, Social Services or an intermediary service. A third party was generally involved who offered support or counselling and a sensitive method of contacting the child, who had to be over eighteen. The urge to reconnect was tempered by the lengthy process which built in contemplation time. The learning cycle of doing, reflecting, theorising and planning next steps was followed. A quick fix was not possible. Reflection, consequences, possible scenarios explored. The needs and situation of the adult adoptee were factored into the process.

Facebook facilitates the quick fix. Social networking allows birth parents to search and reconnect at the touch of a button, without reflection, support or considering the impact on the child and adoptive family. The need to reduce their pain is their paramount driver. Why wouldn't a birth parent send that message?

Independent support for birth parents

Birth parents need support and help processing their grief after their children have been removed. This can't be done by the organisation who took their child away. For the birth parent, that organisation is totally contaminated. Currently the bulk of the counselling and support offered is by post adoption teams within Social Services. They may be different people to the front line staff who decided to remove her child, but from the birth mother's perspective, they are contaminated. They are just another set of social workers in similar rooms, with similar chairs within the same local authority; the same bastards who stole her child. Of course she won't seek help from them, they, in drama triangle terms, are her perpetrators. She needs a new fresh rescuer, but one with the skills, knowledge and judgement to guide her on a path to healing and resolution.

Birth families need access to an independent support service, where they will not feel judged and where specially trained counsellors, therapists or coaches can help them process their grief, trauma and historical baggage. This service could be regional or national, run by a government agency or from within the charity sector. Some funding from central government would be required.

If birth parents can, with time, understand why their children were removed and that their child is getting a fresh start in life, then many birth parents are likely to be more co-operative and sensitive to their child's needs. This may result in healthy, facilitated contact rather than intrusions via social networking. This benefits the child and both sets of parents.

Before readers dismiss this as another costly intervention, just remember the financial cost of keeping a child in the care system. If birth mothers were able to process their grief and trauma, some might stop delivering babies annually which are then repeatedly removed by Social Services and placed in foster care.

An independent support service for birth families must have close working ties with the organisations providing facilitated contact. Again this would benefit all three corners of the adoption triangle and reduce some of the problems created by social networking.

CHAPTER SEVENTEEN

THE ADOPTER'S PERSPECTIVE

*"Living with traumatised children is probably the longest, most challenging,
most stressful task that any adult ever undertakes."*
Dr Mary Mather

Becoming a parent changes most adults; some radically as your values shift and what's truly important to you changes forever.

Parenting children traumatised children transforms the adults who undertake the task, sometimes in a good way. Delivering both the art and science of therapeutic reparenting is exhausting emotionally, physically and spiritually. If you only use 'normal parenting strategies', living with maltreated children is shattering: literally and metaphorically. Their rage can be explosive and destructive; violence to objects, people, pets and themselves all too frequent. Their survival strategies often include crazy lying, hyper-vigilance, stealing and self-sabotaging behaviour. Exclusion or expulsion from school is common, or they may just truant or refuse to attend.

In the midst of this chaos, adoptive parents try to hold a safe space, keep boundaries, nurture and provide a loving home. Year after year. They will also try to hold down a job, possibly parent other children, be a supportive sister, son or friend, pay the bills, cope with family bereavement, flu or something more life threatening. Year after year. Many will have stopped trying to have a 'normal life' because it's just too difficult. Organising industrial-strength babysitters is tricky, so parents find their social life curtailed or non-existent. Year after year.

Daily they are walking on egg shells to avoid triggering an outburst, tantrum or an emotional shutdown from their child. Yet so many adopters hang on in and spend hours helping, supporting, nurturing; filling in the developmental gaps whenever possible, physically holding their children as they sob hysterically, sometimes for hours. Then they may need to listen to the abuse memory or the recounting of a ghastly event. This was cathartic and healing for the child, but how did it impact the adoptive parent? What does it do to them, year after year?

I've heard many adopters say they feel as if they live in a war zone. The problem with a war zone is you don't know when the next attack will come, from where, or the scale of the assault. All you can do is be vigilant because you know it will come. Imagine living like this year after year, with hyper-vigilance your base line state.

During adolescence when hormones kick in things generally get worse.

Some of the abusive events a child experienced were at the hands of a birth mother or father. Many of the child's unmet developmental needs result from the toxic parenting inflicted by a birth parent.

An amalgamated story

Jamie was hurt by his birth mother Alison who drank while pregnant, often left him tied in the buggy when she went on a 'night out' which sometimes became a lengthy drinking binge. Alison often became abusive and violent when drunk. However when sober she appeared meek and cooperative. Social workers took eighteen months to piece the picture together, but only after a neighbour phoned the police who found Jamie tied into his buggy facing the wall.

Pam has spent twelve years parenting Jamie. His executive functioning and emotional intelligence are impaired, probably through a combination of the prenatal alcohol damage, the trauma of being alone for huge chunks of time and living with a frightening and frightened mother.

Pam fought to get Jamie a statement of special educational needs. She often wears long sleeves to cover the bruises on her arms because he hits her. She tried to get therapy for Jamie but was turned down. She asked Social Services for help, but they could offer nothing but sympathy, no adoption support. Sorry, budget constraints don't you know!

Pam does what so many adopters do. She has made the best of it. She has sacrificed much in her own life to parent Jamie. Her days, weeks and months are spent tending his demanding behaviour. Year after year.

Pam knows that Alison is to blame for most of Jamie's problems. Alison neglected Jamie. Alison failed to protect Jamie. Alison repeatedly promised Social Services she would change. Alison is culpable.

Pam also knows Alison had a difficult childhood and many of her own traumas. Pam has some sympathy and compassion for Alison. However she is also angry that Alison hurt *her son, her Jamie*. Pam's protective maternal instinct is enraged by Alison the perpetrator. Pam is also infuriated that Jamie is taking all his anger out on her not Alison. Alison caused the damage, Pam suffers the retribution.

This pattern of a birth parent causing the damage, the child suffering the consequences and the adoptive parents receiving the retribution is played out in many adoptive families. This is the adopter's lot. They didn't cause the damage, but they suffer the reprisals and consequences. Year after year.

Jamie and Alison are both on Facebook. They connected. Within a few days they exchanged mobile numbers, text frequently and spoke several times. Jamie didn't tell Pam.

Imagine how Pam feels when she does find out. The initial devastating shock, anger and sense of helplessness. It's yet another emotional rollercoaster, but completely unexpected and totally out of her control. This one is different; it feels like a dagger through her heart. Her pain is intensely personal. She is devastated. The betrayal and secrecy wound her deeply. Her entire sense of self and of being a mother is shaken to the core.

Pam's imagination runs riot, she fears that Jamie will reconnect and prefer his birth mother to her. She's terrified she might lose her son to his mother. The dread that Alison will let Jamie down again. What state is Alison in, is she still an alcoholic? What if Alison just turns up on the doorstep. What impact will all this have on Jamie's forthcoming exams?

Expectations
Adoptive parents knew that their children might reconnect with members of their birth family, but they expected it to be in adulthood, facilitated and considered. Most adopters support their children in the search and reunion process. Adopters don't expect the reconnection during the turbulent teenage years. They don't expect birth family to enter their homes via Facebook or texts. This is unsupervised contact with no boundaries or rules.

For adopters it is a terrifying prospect.

It is too early to know the long-term outcome of these reconnections and the subsequent relationships between adopters and their children. However, anecdotal evidence is that some adopters have 'lost' their children (as teenagers or young adults) to birth parents. In a bizarre parallel with the birth parents' situation, adopters are now "parents without children" and going through a grieving process. Will that change with time? Will these adolescents search out their adoptive parents as they reach their late twenties or thirties? We will have to wait and see.

Adopters place in the community

If they have stayed in the same home for a number of years, adoptive parents probably have many acquaintances met through or with their children. What does an adopter say when chatting to a parent they knew from primary school days? The conversation is inevitably focussed around their children's lives. How does an adopter answer direct, probing questions? Sharing the truth is not appropriate, it's confidential, so again an adopter will wriggle to avoid sharing secrets and possibly cross the road to avoid such a conversation. I know I have.

Just like birth parents, the losses as a consequence of adoption are with the adoptive parents forever.

Anecdotes

The remainder of this chapter is adopters' stories in their own unedited words. Only identifying details have been changed. I am deeply grateful to these individuals for allowing their words and experiences to be heard unfiltered. Remember their real lives continue; these people will continue living the story you read. Who knows what the outcomes will be a year from now, this is real life, not fiction.

Anecdote 1: An email correspondence

FEB 2011. An experience to add to the many you have doubtless already heard. Our daughter contacted her birth family through Facebook in September last year when she was just 16. The effect has been of dropping a large boulder into the little pool that was our family. She has met both birth parents, and 3 siblings, one of whom is also formally adopted, and has had direct news of 3 more siblings, the existence of 2 of which was previously unknown to us. None remained with the birth parents (only one shares the same father as our daughter). One sibling is dead. Our daughter has absconded from home frequently, dropped out of college, lost numerous personal possessions, subjected us to a tide of verbal abuse (although she says she doesn't want to hurt us; but she was never an easy child) and caused her adopted brother also to go into meltdown. It has been an extremely stressful rollercoaster. The police have been involved on several occasions (daughter missing x 2, son being violent x 1, flat of birth sister trashed by boyfriend). We feel numb, abandoned, no idea where we are going to wash up. My husband and I press on a day at a time because that is all you can do. Some days we are very close to breaking point.

SEPT 2011. Thank you. After a very slow start on the part of the agencies, social services have now managed to engage with a (very) reluctant daughter, and she has had one session with the clinical psychologist, more to come. She is still at home (mostly) although we have had some horrendous days along the way. She is still talking to (at) us, and occasionally she is not shouting, and even smiles. So I guess things are a little better. She has no college place or job, although I believe she may have applied for one in Tescos in the last day or two. Her level of maturity seems to have regressed to about age seven to ten.

As you say, if there was a road map, and I knew eventually we would emerge from the other side, I could cope better. I have had to learn to let go of all the things you hope for, with a child; that they will be safe, that they will come home, that they will show you some affection, and finally, bonus of bonuses, that they will achieve sufficient skills to make their own way in life. Forget A levels, sports skills, university, all those things 'normal' parents hope for, they are long gone (even though they were all within her reach, once). I am in tsunami survivor mode now; just glad no-one's nicked my blanket in the communal sleeping station. Tiny things make me happy (like she has actually texted before 10.30pm to say spending night at birth father's (a horrible place that I prefer not to think about...) My husband and I are trying to care for ourselves, but it's tough. We have some very good friends, and a crowd of USELESS relatives who have mostly been no help at all. And as for the state education system....considering they are in the business of educating children, they seem to know very little about them.

Really feel Facebook is very culpable here, and may have completely changed the face of adoption for the future. I for one would not, I think, consider it now, knowing what I know.

An adoptive mother

Written on request: Anecdote 2
Our daughter was placed with us from the care system when she was eight.

At the age of six, she and her younger brother had been removed from their birth parents due to neglect and physical and emotional abuse and placed in separate foster families.

It was clear from the start that she had been traumatised by her early experiences in her birth family and that this early trauma had impacted on all areas of her physical, emotional and cognitive development. In reality, this meant that she looked and behaved like a child of five and was barely able to read or write.

Over time, she started to settle down in our family and to grow at an amazing rate! With extra support in primary and secondary education and with our continued help and support, she made significant progress in all areas and her self-esteem improved.

BUBBLE WRAPPED CHILDREN

As adopters of an older child, who had lived with her birth parents for six years, we were aware from the outset of the need to acknowledge the birth family's continuing importance and presence in our daughter's life. When she felt the need, we talked openly to her about her birth family and maintained annual letterbox contact with her birth parents, even though this proved to be a one-way process.

Although we had been warned that problems could arise in the teenage years, by the start of her GCSE year, our daughter had grown into a confident 15 year old who was managing to keep up with her peers and was busily preparing for her forthcoming exams. Then just weeks before her 16th Birthday and the start of her GCSEs, she was traced by her birth family via Facebook, shaking us all to the core and threatening the very foundations of the family unit we had worked so hard to build.

Just 48 hours after this unsolicited contact from her birth family, our daughter was in regular touch with her birth mother by mobile 'phone and demanding to see her "blood family". As her GCSEs approached she became increasingly disengaged from learning and from us. It took all our energies to try to keep her focused on her exams. Although we managed to keep her on track, she did not achieve anywhere near the grades she needed to go on to do "A" Levels and is now on a vocational course.

Nearly a year on, we continue to look on helplessly as our daughter exchanges text messages with her birth mother and links up with yet another member of the extended birth family. There is no acknowledgement on the part of the birth parents of why she was removed from them or of the damage this caused her. She has disconnected from us completely. We are trying to arrange facilitated contact with her birth parents, but this is proving difficult to achieve.

Recently, our daughter has linked up with a crowd of new friends whom we have never met and has also started smoking and engaging in sexual activity. We have been told that we are one of the luckier families because she has confided in us about the Facebook contact and - as far as we are aware - has not yet met up with her birth parents or worse still, run away from home. When you watch in horror as your vulnerable teenage daughter is derailed in this way, it is of little consolation.

An adoptive mother

Written on request: Anecdote 3

My daughter Ali came to me at 4, a tiny waif, unhappy and oppositional. She left home at 17, big and strong but still oppositional, blaming me for the relationship breakdown, unable to see that all her relationships failed. Drugs and alcohol became a big part of her life and we, her adoptive parents, a source of money and occasional meals.

At 20 she reconnected with her birth mother on Facebook. Two years on, her name, not mine, features on Ali's Facebook front page as "mother". All her friends can see this very public change of status.

In the last five years I have received no Mother's Day or birthday cards. My role in her life has been dismissed and I am ignored. I feel very hurt and sometimes wonder whether all my efforts over 13 years, to mother her were wasted. I have nothing to show for all my efforts. Am I bitter? Probably. My friends meet their daughters for lunch or shopping trips, some are planning weddings, while others are delighting in grandparenthood. I will never have those joys.

An adoptive mother

Written on request: Anecdote 4

Our two adopted girls are sisters, the eldest of a group of four. Their two younger brothers were also adopted together. As the girls hit their early teens twice-yearly face-to-face contact became more testing for the other family. The girls led their brothers into trouble at contact, behaved aggressively towards me and loved showing off their 'coolness' with their bad language. Unsurprisingly the other family called off contact. This was not the example that they needed to be set for their young boys.

The girls were devastated to lose contact after all those years, and delighted when they were able to make contact with the elder boy through Facebook. Of course, their exploits – sex, drugs and rock and roll - interests were posted all over their Facebook accounts. Very soon the other adopters realised and broke off all Facebook contact too. Who could blame them? Yet we had two youngsters suffering rejection yet again. It is only a matter of time before the brothers and sisters hook up again.

Meanwhile, the placement has partially disrupted. The older girl is in foster care nearby and the younger in a specialist residential home a couple of hours away. Not long after the younger one moved, one of her friends advised me of the 'plan'. Through Facebook the elder sister had recruited a whole team of friends of hers and her sister, and had devised a plan to travel en masse to the younger one's home in the south of England and spring her out (a couple of the group had cars). Through

BUBBLE WRAPPED CHILDREN

Facebook they had identified an adult male in Scotland (not directly known to them) who they believed would hide the younger one for 18 months. They had not posted anything on Facebook directly, but handled everything through Facebook chat and messages which was not seen. A far-fetched scheme of course, but one they were committed to carrying out, if not thwarted by myself and professionals involved.

We have a high level of contact with the younger child, who will increasingly be coming home for holidays and weekends. Since all the changes her attachment to us has really come to the fore. She has handmade the most beautiful Christmas card for me, bought us presents from her pocket money, and can't hug us enough or get any closer when we see her. Just this week I have done the four hour round trip just to be with her at the dentist, as she 'can't have a filling unless Mum's with me'. Yet still she is searching Facebook constantly for her birth family, just as her sister is. They are teens now, grappling with issues of identity, trying to understand the past and deal with the enormous conflict of loving and wanting birth Mum whilst knowing she let them down. They are awaiting formal channels of contact, but the system moves far too slow. Meanwhile the search for all family members on Facebook continues unabated. I wait with bated breath. One day the search will succeed and unstructured, unfiltered contact will happen, birth Mum may be saint or devil, and we will be trying to handle the fallout.

An adoptive mother

"If you're going through hell, keep going."
Winston Churchill

CHAPTER EIGHTEEN

WHAT'S HAPPENING NOW

It's impossible to gauge what percentage of adopted children are actively looking for members of their birth family and its equally difficult to know what percentage of birth parents are actively seeking children removed from them by the courts.

Similarly we can't know the long-term consequences of the connections already made. However from the existing evidence we can predict likely scenarios and from that draw up an action plan and strategies.

Adoption numbers and statistics
In the last decade (2000-2010) within the England and Wales, roughly 3,000 and 4,000 children were adopted from the Care system, of which, according to UK Government Statistics, 40-60% of adoptions were for children between one and four, while 25-32% of adoptions were for five to nine-year-olds.) The average age of children being adoption reduced during this decade.

In the previous decade, 1990-2000, the numbers were slightly higher, while in 1980 the number of children adopted was 10,609, dropping to 6,533 in 1990. However drawing conclusions from the bald data over thirty years is unwise as it is unclear how many children were adopted from the care system and how many by step parents. So calculating the number of adoptees who might be reconnected with members of their birth family is tricky. However in rough terms, it's "quite a lot".

The scale of the Facebook/adoption issue past, present and future
The vast majority of children adopted between 1990 and 2000 will now be adolescents. That is in excess of 30,000 probably between 35,000 and 40,000 adoptees, between the ages of twelve and twenty-five-ish for whom Facebook is transforming their life within their adoptive family right now.

This issue will affect every secondary school in the country. Statistically there will be at least one adolescent adoptee in every year group throughout the UK. Schools will need some sensitivity and understanding around the shadow side of social networking. While cyber bullying is recognised as an issue, reconnecting to members of birth family brings a whole new dimension.

BUBBLE WRAPPED CHILDREN

For children adopted between 2000 and 2010, some are now in early adolescence, a few in mid adolescence. This is roughly another 30,000 children who will be reconnected with their birth families via social networking over the next few years.
These statistics are purely for England and Wales. That is over 65,000 adolescents and young adult adoptees who have the potential to reconnect with members of their birth family at the touch of a button. Many of them already have. This phenomenon is not restricted to the UK. This is a global issue, touching tens of thousands of adopted children, because the underlying issues for most birth parents and adoptees are the same.

Inter-country adoptions are not included in the numbers. However, inter-country adoptees will be touched by the technological shrinking of the world and may have some unique issues and dilemmas which are raised at the end of the chapter.

What about infants being adopted right now, next month or next year? What about the children not yet conceived? Children adopted during the 2010s have the possibility of vaccination using adoption support, therapeutic reparenting, truth telling, therapy and possibly facilitated contact. These children could be the beneficiaries from the fallout because it forces a redesigning of the entire adoption model.

Who is looking?
Δ Some children are looking for birth parents
Δ Some birth parents are looking for children
Δ Some birth family children are looking for siblings who were adopted
Δ Some adopted children are looking for siblings who were not adopted
Δ Some adopted children are looking for siblings who were adopted by another family
Δ Some siblings, aunts, uncles, grandparents and birth family friends are looking for adopted children.

Sometimes the "looking" is just curiosity: *"could I find her if I looked?"* Other times it is an active intense search with the definite intent of reconnecting. Occasionally it's a drunken late night internet trawl, regretted in the morning. Anecdotal evidence, reinforced by statistics, is that Facebook is currently the favoured platform. With over 30 million users in the UK, (population around 62 million) and over 750 million worldwide, Facebook is used by almost half of the UK population and over 10% of the world's population. That includes all ages, so you can draw your own conclusions about its use by younger people. Facebook has a minimum age of thirteen for opening an account; however many younger children simply put in a false year of birth, but keep the correct day and month.

"43% of 9 to 12 year-olds in Britain have a profile on a social networking site."
The Guardian Newspaper 23 April 2011

How are they looking?

The methods of looking and searching vary, but with simply a date of birth, a first name, country and some patience it is possible to locate someone on the internet. If you know a common link, such as an old foster parent or school, finding someone is easy. Sending an email to a hundred people that says "Hello I think I am your mum" is likely to be ignored by ninety-nine recipients, but it only needs to hit the one intended target and the goal is reached.

Other methods have proved simpler. If an adopted child connects to a member of the old foster family, then birth parents can find them instantly. Name tags on photographs can be used to locate people. There are a wide variety of methods, which might change daily, could change weekly, probably change monthly and will definitely change annually. Technological advances and user interface upgrades are designed for social network sites prime aims: to connect people and share data. That is their core business.

Being "found" is unavoidable unless either your level of protection is immense because you keep constantly abreast of hourly technological changes or you have no online presence. Bluntly, if someone wants to find you online, they have the time and some technical competence, they will. For parents who are now thinking they can stop adolescents using the internet and social networking, dream on. Kids can access the internet at school, on their phones and at friend's houses. Living inside a social networking-free bubble is impossible.

How are they reconnecting?

The evidence about methods and speed of hooking up is anecdotal; however all of the following have occurred as a response to an online "hello".

- Δ Nothing at all. One person may send an email via Facebook but the recipient chooses not to respond at all and does not respond to further "Hellos" or more emotionally charged emails.
- Δ The online response is delayed
- Δ The online response is immediate
- Δ The connection results in exchanging mobile phone numbers
- Δ The connection results in an immediate phone call
- Δ The connection results in a face-to-face meeting within days or weeks
- Δ Some reconnections occur with the knowledge of the adoptive parents
- Δ Some adoptees eventually tell their adoptive parents
- Δ Some adoptees never tell their adoptive parents

Remember contact works when birth parents:
- Δ Take responsibility and offer a coherent account of what life was like for the child when living with them
- Δ Say "sorry", it was our fault not yours.
- Δ Give blessing to where the child is currently living

These criteria and the deeper reasoning explained in Chapter 14 are not being followed when reconnecting via Facebook. *Dher.* After the initial contact there are numerous possible outcomes which the reader can conjure for themselves. Some outcomes are surprising or shocking. Many adoptees have been thrown into emotional disarray by the reconnection, even when they instigated the search, because whatever the response, it shakes them to their core.

What happened next?
The following have all happened to real families and real children.
- Δ After the initial one-to-one reconnection, an array of birth family members and new partners also connect. Suddenly the adoptee is in contact, virtually and/or physically with a large extended family. In some cases this has included family members who abused the child
- Δ After an initial enthusiastic exchange of emails and texts, one side withdraws from the new relationship, leaving the other confused and hurt. This can result in the sending of abusive messages demanding reconnection
- Δ After an initial enthusiastic exchange of emails and texts, a meeting is suggested, but birth family members repeatedly find reasons to postpone and so disappoint the adoptee
- Δ Individual members of sibling groups have differed in their response to the birth parent's reappearance, ranging from delight to horror This has affected their relationship, especially when the birth parent enlists the help of the "cooperative" sibling to influence the "uncooperative" sibling
- Δ A birth parent clearly favoured one child over another after reconnection
- Δ Meetings have been planned and implemented without the adoptive parents knowing
- Δ Birth parents are denying the abuse and neglect happened and demanding the child concurs
- Δ A sixteen-year-old teenage adoptee leaves the adoptive home and moves in with a "reasonable" birth mother.
- Δ The adoptee is so disturbed just by receiving the email that he drops out of university and slides into depression and a vodka bottle

Δ The teenage adoptee leaves the adoptive home and moves in with a highly dysfunctional birth family who have had all their many children removed social services. The police are frequent visitors

Δ Adoptees discover their faces and photographs on birth parents' websites or Facebook pages

Δ A teenage adoptee has connected to older siblings who stayed with the birth family. These young adults abuse drugs and alcohol with all the accompanying by products. The adoptee has fallen into "rescue mode"

Δ Birth parents declined to participate in facilitated contact with a third party

Δ Throughout the country many teenagers have their schooling impacted; exams are missed and course work not completed after unexpected emails from birth family

Ramifications of unplanned reconnection

For adopted children, their birth family had values, standards, expectations and behaviours which caused the courts to permanently remove them. These birth parents were not able to put the child's needs ahead of their own, often inflicting chaos and pain. The child did not feel safe.

By contrast, adopters and foster carers have been vetted, trained and approved by an external agency before they were allowed to parent children. They provide child-centred nurturing and stability, a parenting model with values, expectations and behaviours that reflect those of mainstream society.

This conundrum is crucial when parenting children from the care system. The acceptance of the birth family shadow is a prerequisite when approving adopters. Birth parents are, and always will be, incredibly important to the child for many reasons. However, Facebook brings that shadow into the foreground and shoves it into a child's face via a computer screen.

This raises huge internal conflict for the child. They have been 'found'. Their secure base fractured. Their physiological stress responses will heighten, their behaviour becomes more challenging; they will compare adopters and birth family; they will resent adopters who, in contrast to most birth families, hold secure behavioural boundaries. Even more battles will occur in the adoptive family home.

How can a child feel safe when pulled in two directions? When home doesn't feel like a safe space, not only is healing impaired but extra conflict is generated. The therapeutic reparenting is interrupted, possibly for years.

The Big Question: "What's changed?"

What has changed within the birth family in the intervening years between a child being removed and then reconnecting with the birth family?

Have the reasons a child was removed been addressed?

Which members of the birth family pose a threat to the adopted child and which might enhance their lives? Which can be honest about the past and create a fulfilling relationship and which will simply continue from where they left off?

How have each of the players changed? Siblings will now be teenagers or young adults themselves. What are their perspectives, motivations and circumstances? Are these siblings doing the searching?

What do you think might happen in the following scenarios?

1. What if at the time of the adoptive placement a birth mother was addicted to crack cocaine, her home chaotic, grime ridden, populated by other junkies, the classic 'drug den', and her priority satisfying the drug habit; is she now clean? If so, for how long? Where does she live and with whom? Does she have a job, interests, hobbies? Has she exchanged drugs for alcohol abuse? Is there a succession of men in her life? How many other children has she borne? How many are still with her? What sort of parent is she?

2. What if the birth father was a classic drunk, who was okay when sober but returned from the pub or drinking binge wielding his fists, shouting and smashing furniture? He created a terrifying environment, heavy with the threat of domestic violence. What if this man has been attending Alcoholics Anonymous meetings for the last eleven years, been sober for a decade and held down a good job for nine years?

3. Stan, the oldest brother in the birth family, looked after his two younger sisters when his parents were incapacitated. He loved them deeply. He cared for them, fed them, played with them and protected them from their parent's rage, often using his own body to shield the blows. Stan remained with his birth parents after his sisters, aged three and four, were removed and later adopted. He has a volatile relationship with his parents and no other family. Stan is desperate to find out how Amy and Sarah are doing. Stan also has "anger issues", often fuelled by drinking binges.

4. The birth mother, whose mental health problems and psychotic behaviour were a major factor in the removal of a child, may now have support from the local psychiatric nurse and follow a prescribed drug regime, so she now lives a "normal" life. How will she respond to unexpected contact from the birth child she barely remembers? Will it destabilise her fragile mental health? What support will she need?

5. Consider the birth father whose "little princess" was removed because he was a practising, but not convicted, paedophile wants to reconnect with his daughter. Has he addressed his paedophilia? Has he spent years working with a therapist specialising in treating such men? Does he use the internet to satisfy his lust for children? Other than sexually abusing her, this man treated his daughter with kindness, showered her with presents and lovely day trips. Yes, the possibility of rape was always present, but it "only happened one weekend in three". Seventeen years later, this "little princess" has a fully formed adult body. What danger does he pose to her? What risk to her unborn child?

6. Emma was three years older than her twin brothers and adopted separately. At nineteen she has little contact with her adoptive parents but sees her birth mother frequently. Emma desperately wants to see herself, her brothers and mother reunited. She searches Facebook, finds them and immediately and sends an email. The brothers receive it the night before their first GCSE exam. Gary is excited and responds immediately giving his mobile phone number. Tom is scared that his birth mum will hurt him again and wants nothing to do with her. Gary wants to tell their adoptive parents. Tom doesn't. The boys argue.

Each of these above scenarios are based on true cases; reconstructed to protect individual identities. The following have not, to my knowledge, happened, but they might:

1. A young man knocks on the adoptive parent's front door asking to come in. They have not seen him for a decade. He walked out aged sixteen to live with his birth family:
    a. He is drunk and aggressive. How should they respond?
    b. He is dishevelled and appears unwell. How should they respond?
    c. He is accompanied by his five-year-old son whom they knew nothing about. How should they respond?
2. Ali's mother's trial was high profile and reported graphically by the media. Her surname, Rhys-Smith-Patel, is unusual. An internet search by Ali details

159

much of the abuse he suffered at her hands. Several years ago Ali told his best mate in strict confidence. They recently had a huge fight and his mate posted a message on Ali's Facebook page saying, "You are evil just like your mum, Mrs Rhys-Smith-Patel."

3. Mai receives an email originating from the country of her birth asking her about her new life.

4. Jo has reconnected with her birth father without telling her adoptive parents. Her birth father is threatening to visit Jo at home unless she gives him money. Jo is terrified.

5. Ellie meets a member of her birth family who kidnaps her.

6. Lia receives an email originating from the country of her birth. The sender says he is her cousin writing on behalf of her mother who is ill and requires an operation and expensive drugs. Can she please send some money otherwise her mother will die.

7. Alex discovers his mother and sister were killed by his birth father.

Some readers may think these scenarios and case studies are exaggerated. I wish they were. The blunt truth is that many individuals who had children adopted have changed little in the intervening years. A significant number of birth mothers have a succession of children, most or all of whom are adopted or fostered. These women do not seem to learn or change. Their executive function skills, empathy and parenting capacity is fixed at a low level. Reunification will not bring the fairy tale ending for any corner of the adoption triangle. While writing this book I heard stories far worse than the scenarios I envisaged, which if recounted here, some readers simply would not believe. Truth is often stranger than fiction.

Pattern detection
Patterns of common behaviour amongst adoptees will emerge after reconnection; however it is much too early to know what they are and the story is only partly written. Patterns emerge with time, volume and the space to analyse and reflect on the findings. These patterns are important because their findings should be feed back into social work practice, care planning, parenting, training for professionals, foster carers and adopters and national policy formation.

One anecdotal pattern currently emerging is how some adoptees refer to their adoptive parents and birth parents. A significant number are reclassifying their adoptive parents by referring to them by their first names, while birth mothers become "Mum". Sometimes only one parent is renamed. As this is indicative of an adoptees claiming behaviour, thinking, belief system and core identity; it will be fascinating to track this over time. Will some revert back? Time will tell.

PART 3: PIECING IT ALL TOGETHER

*"When man wanted to make a machine
that would walk, he created a wheel,
which did not resemble a leg."*
Guillaume Apollinaire

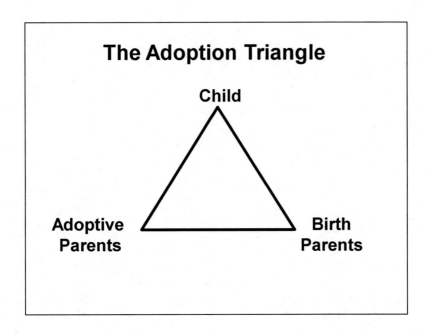

The Adoption Triangle

Child

Adoptive
Parents

Birth
Parents

CHAPTER NINETEEN

CRISIS, OPPORTUNITY OR THREAT?

"Not everything that counts can be counted, and not everything that can be counted counts."
Albert Einstein

Law of unintended consequences

The law of unintended consequences is a neat little idea which suggests that there are generally three types of unplanned outcomes resulting from a purposeful action.

Δ Positive unexpected benefit

Δ Negative unexpected detriment

Δ Perverse contrary effect: actions which cause the opposite of what was intended

Facebook ethos

As anyone who has seen the film The Social Network will know; the impact of their computer system on adoption (or anything else) was not on the radar of the Facebook creators. Their focus was very different, supremely adolescent and testosterone driven. Neither Henry Ford nor Bill Gates could anticipate the joys, difficulties, challenges or worldwide transformation their products would bring. We don't blame Ford for car accidents or Gates for internet pornography, however we might curse them when our car won't start or our laptop crashes.

The same principle is true for the transformation of adoption by Facebook. Blaming Facebook for providing the opportunity for unsupervised contact is missing the point. There was always the desire; Facebook simply provided a neat method to achieve clumsy results.

Facebook intended to connect people, but did not, or could not, foresee the consequences. It's worth just pausing and reminding ourselves that Facebook was only launched in February 2004, and first opened to anyone aged over thirteen with an email address in September 2006. The entire world has been transformed by Facebook, social media and social networking. The Arab Spring in Tunisia, Egypt and Libya being global positives; adoption is just one arena where there have been massive unintended negative consequences. There is no light without shadow, change always bring unintended consequences.

BUBBLE WRAPPED CHILDREN

The Facebook business model, and those of other social media sites, is to encourage people to share and distribute the maximum amount of information. Their professional game is full disclosure, not confidentiality. Social networking is a perfect gossip vehicle. Paste something on your wall and instantly hundreds of people hear it through that grapevine: if it's juicy and worth retelling, probably thousands. The onus is on individual members to decide what to share. This business model is highly profitable. It ain't gonna change, but it will get replicated.

Facebook users must protect their own privacy and confidentiality but have no control on what others say about them. Once a piece of data is posted, it is there forever, so old muddy gossip is always available for the aggrieved to throw. Adolescents seldom think about the future, so are vulnerable to the "post now, regret later" syndrome plus revenge can be instantaneous and vicious. All this is true for any adolescent. Adopted, fostered abused and vulnerable teenagers have so much more to lose.

OMG: How many users?
In May 2007 there were 23 million Facebook users worldwide. Staggeringly, within thirty-two months that was the number of users within just the UK. Currently the number of UK Facebook users is about half of the UK population.

Timings	Number of Facebook Users in UK	Number of Facebook Users Worldwide
December 2006	1.35 million	12 million
May 2007	3.5 million	23 million
February 2008	8.5 million	60 million
January 2009	17.6 million	150 million
December 2009	23 million	350 million
August 2010	24.2 million	520 million
September 2011	30 million	750 million

With such exponential growth it is impossible for adoption or fostering to keep pace with the impact of these huge technological changes. Many commercial companies struggle to surf the social media wave. To expect Social Service departments, foster carers or adoptive parents to "control" this technology is ridiculous. The solution has to come from a different direction.

Other social media, social networking and businesses will develop on the internet. Google have entered the field, others will invent new applications. It is impossible to

164

predict. We have to deal with the root cause not the symptom. Empower the child rather than fiddle around with privacy settings.

Facebook has phased in a new user interface, Facebook Timeline, which will enable users to access their historical content and fill in their life experiences on a digital timeline retrospectively, with photographs, videos and key life events. People will have the opportunity to share their stories not only with those who are in their lives now, but also with the generations to come by creating a digital and historical footprint. The ramifications for children who have been through the care system is huge and from the confidentiality angle most alarming.

We don't know what will be happening technologically seven months from now; let alone seven years from now. However we do know that children who experienced maltreatment in infancy will have trauma triggered behaviour, they would benefit from therapy which helps them process 100% of their life story truthfully, and birth parents will want some contact. Therefore we must empower the adopted and fostered child and the parents with whom they live.

Collective crisis: opportunity or threat?
The advent and growth of social networking and global connectivity offers a fantastic opportunity to redesign the adoption model. We have a choice: either redesign and improve the adoption model in the light of contact via social networking and enhance adoption for all parties or leave things as they are. With only a tweak here and there, we will watch adoptive placements fall apart during early, middle and late adolescence, while adopter recruitment dwindles to just a handful of unimaginative adults, and adoption as we know it simply evaporates.

No change = no prospective adopters
We are in the midst of a crisis, which the Chinese denote by combining the two symbols of danger and opportunity. There is immense danger to the very existence of adoption if nothing changes. What sensible prospective adopter would take on a child knowing that unsupervised, direct contact between their son and the birth parents who maltreated him would occur as he hit his teens? What enlightened prospective adopter would want to be matched to a child whose birth parents have zero degrees of empathy, are violently opposed to the adoption and tell social workers "I'll find my kid and get him back"? Adopters expect to have their child in their life, for life, not a mere decade. Their dreams include a lengthy time line as an integrated adoptive family. However, post Facebook expecting adopters to take children, as if nothing has changed is basically offering fostering without payment, but with all the legal parental responsibilities. A lose/lose situation and grossly unfair to all parties.

If an adopted child hooks up with the birth family, then refuses to attend school or gets in trouble with the police, it is the adoptive parents who are legally responsible and expected to pay for damage, guarantee court appearances, school attendance and other such delights. The adopters probably have little control over the child, no means of enacting or enforcing rules, yet they will be punished by the law for any violation. That is already happening. All the adopters can do is hold up their hands and say *"s/he is out of my control and needs to be taken into care. We relinquish our parental responsibility"*. The child then re-enters the care system. Statistically, not an adoption breakdown, but in reality a set of devastated adopters who have lost their child to birth parents who can resume contact with the child but take no responsibility. What self-respecting prospective adopters will knowingly set themselves up for that kind of pain? Existing adopters with children in place have no choice. Prospective adopters do.

Prospective adopters would be mad to accept a child under these circumstances, because they are setting themselves up to fail.

Prospective adopters will need to accept that ongoing therapy and disclosure work will be part of their lives as an adoptive family. In many cases this will include ongoing facilitated contact with the birth family.

Trust issues (reliability + credibility + intimacy ÷ self-interest)
Prospective adopters must insist that ongoing therapy, disclosure work and facilitated contact is part of their adoption support package. That plan must be in writing and legally robust. Verbal promises are useless. Many adopters have experienced those from social workers and managers, who at the time, genuinely meant it, but an organisational restructure, change of staff or political direction, resulted in the withdrawal of the promised support. This happens nationally too.

I have been a regular attendee at the All Party Parliamentary Adoption Group meetings in Westminster for a decade. Several years ago I witnessed the incumbent minister renege on promises about adoption support made by previous ministers. My two related questions were dismissed as an irrelevance. An MP picked up the issue, reiterating the earlier government promises. We were told, in effect, "I am now the minister; I make the decisions and am not responsible for earlier promises made by members of my own party holding this office." It was scandalous, arrogant behaviour which broke trust between adoptive parents, adoption professionals and decision makers. Other ministers have behaved honourably, but it only takes one rogue decision maker at national or local level for promises, hopes and children's lives to be shattered.

For senior managers and politicians groaning at the content of these paragraphs, compare therapeutic intervention to the cost of foster care, secure units, prisons and vandalism. It's a no brainer. Early interventions make the most difference, but appropriate support is needed until maturity. Children in foster care have ongoing support until twenty-one – why not adopted children?

Individual crisis: no change = teenagers return

If nothing changes, adolescent adoptees will reconnect to their birth families who are likely to have a very different value system to their adoptive parents. Birth parents may offer an escape route for the troubled teenager and the adoptive placement collapse as the adolescent refuses to abide by the adopter's rules and value system. The reunification with the birth family may temporarily 'work', because the birth family offer an attractive lifestyle which appeals to the adolescent. Their sense of rejection may be diminished and they may feel as if they have genuinely "come home".

However, the *"what has changed question"* applies. Is the teenager safe? Are any boundaries applied? What behaviour is acceptable? Does that behaviour comply with the views of society? What is expected and what is not? What is condoned and what is encouraged. Will the child attend school, college or get employment? How will the child's internal working model, internal body knowledge and sense of self handle the conflicting information given by birth parents who deny maltreatment? Are drugs, alcohol or promiscuity promoted, tolerated or discouraged?

If during childhood the adopted child has not had the opportunity to resolve his infancy trauma and maltreatment, then his layers of protective bubble wrap will still be in place. His birth family could be perceived as scary and exciting, familiar and different, attractive and repellent. In short; a very confusing blurred picture.

All of these things were true before social networking intruded, but now a fourteen-year-old adoptee can reconnect to birth parents and already sixteen-year-olds are voting with their feet and returning to live with a birth family, who have not changed since the children were removed. Teenagers are returning to abusive, toxic birth parents. This trend will continue unless dramatic interventions occur. Either we adapt our operational practices or Facebook will destroy adoption as we know it.

The diagram gives some sense of how Facebook reconnections reduce the opportunity for therapeutic reparenting during adolescence thus impacting the 15% brain rewiring which occurs during adolescence.

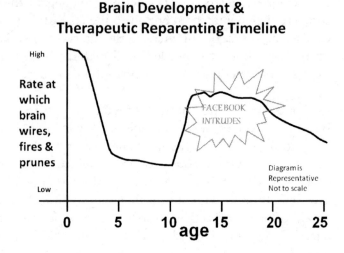

Brain Development & Therapeutic Reparenting Timeline

The impact of adopted children reconnecting with birth family members haphazardly at twelve, fourteen or sixteen or eighteen or twenty is very different from adopted adults reconnecting using a third party when they are older and more mature.

Effect on the individual adoptee

Previously re-establishing contact took into account the situation of each individual. The timing would be sensitive to the current events and challenges in both parties' life. Now an email can arrive during exams, directly after a bereavement, during an illness or some other life crisis. This can tip an adolescent or vulnerable adult over the edge. Already adopted adolescents have "blown" GCSEs, and A-Levels: sometimes after voluntarily reconnecting to birth family or simply by receiving an uninvited email. An unexpected message is enough to make a child feel threatened and unsafe. The consequence of that lack of control is huge: neatly summed up by Darren. *"My biggest fear was always unexpectedly meeting her and then she arrived in my bedroom via my computer screen."* In an instant, his secure, safe base disappeared from under him.

Applying Maslow's Hierarchy of Needs model, Darren's focus of attention dropped from self actualisation and academic pursuits at college into fear-based behaviour which would fulfil his safety needs. He stopped attending classes and social events as he tried to come to terms with this unwelcome intrusion into his life. He became stuck, life around him continued, he missed assignments and dropped out of his college course into depression which he self-medicated with vodka and strong lager. Darren has not chosen to respond to the continuing Facebook emails he receives from his birth mother. However the occasional messages and possibility of her unwelcome presence in his life are a constant source of anxiety for him. The depression and sense of helplessness continues, punctured by outbursts of alcohol-induced aggression. Sadly he is unwilling to address the issue with his adoptive parents or anyone else. Readers may feel that reconnecting with his birth mother might be useful, as she is omnipresent. For Darren it's a Catch 22 and double bind. His biggest fear is seeing her; yet seeing her could reduce his anxiety, but he is too scared to think about doing it, creating a vicious circle.

Anxiety is fear of the future. How much easier would life have been for Darren if this bubble of fear had been slowly depressurised during childhood, rather than building up to the pressure-cooker proportions he is now experiencing? What if there had been facilitated contact between him and the birth mother with whom the thought of reconnection currently terrify him? Would it have reduced his fears? Would that have been enough for the birth mother? Might they have formed a "workable" relationship, by which I mean a relationship which works for both of them? The relationship might be a simple connection, possibly superficial, maybe something more. The current lose/lose/lose situation for all three parties could have been avoided if some facilitated contact had occurred during his childhood. Prevention is better than cure, and cheaper.

Volume and vulnerability
Prior to Facebook, reconnection between adult adoptees and members of their birth family was so much harder, hence the volume was low. Now it's relatively easy. There is a very high chance that curiosity will motivate adopted children to look for birth family members at some point during their adolescence via social networking. Even if a third don't, with over 3,000 children adopted from the care system each year in the UK, it's quite likely that at the very least 40,000 adoptees born in the 1980s and 1990 have looked for members of their birth family via social networking sites. How many of those have reconnected? We just don't know. Adoptees placed this century will certainly look online before they reach adulthood.

Who is looking?
For every adopted child there is a birth family, consisting of parents; probably sisters, brothers, grandparents, aunts, uncles, cousins and possibly new partners and friends. Many children placed for adoption come from quite large birth families with numerous siblings. Some birth mothers have four, six, eight, ten or more children, many of whom were fostered or adopted. So Darren may have older siblings who may want to reconnect and they are searching for him, but have not told their mother.

BUBBLE WRAPPED CHILDREN

There could be numerous people looking for one specific adopted child online yearning to reconnect. An adopted child could suddenly have a dozen or more new relatives wanting to share his life. How does he manage that? Which are safe to reconnect to and who are toxic? Can he connect to some and not others? What are the birth family dynamics? Have some been adopted? A complex tangled web of conflicting feelings, views, history, memories, desires and motivations have materialised in the adoptee's life. Sadly every adoptee has a story like Darren's.

Let's also consider the flip side and recognise that members of the birth family are often highly vulnerable individuals themselves with their own issues, challenges and life crises, whose lives will be transformed by contact via Facebook, whether instigated by them or not. For various birth family members there are probably conflicting feelings and intentions. Some may not want to reconnect; others are desperate to do so. Managing the reconnection congruently to match the desired pace of all participants is impossible. How can this not result in tears? What if the adoptee wants to reconnect to siblings but not birth parents, but the siblings are still living with the birth parents? What if the younger siblings were adopted and in crisis themselves? What if some family members are not speaking to others and the emotions of anger, sadness and resentment fill the air? Truth will be hard to find within such complex family dynamics and when so many people with different aims and objectives attempt to re-establishing contact. Compared to this, soap operas' story lines sound quite tame.

CHAPTER TWENTY

THE BIG PICTURE, A NEW MODEL AND A MINDSET SHIFT

"The real art of discovery is not to visit new lands, but to see existing lands with new eyes."
Marcel Proust

This is the exciting bit; the part where we can turn the threat into a great opportunity. Clearly social networking is transforming adoption as we know it and will continue to do so. By recognising the adoption process as a complex system with many components which vary with time we can start to address the underlying issues and the causes rather than tinker with symptoms.

Systems
A system is a set of interconnecting parts which function as a whole. A heap is a collection of parts. This is not the place to attempting to explain the complexities of the adoption system or the heap of things which make up adoption. While at all stages the intent should be to fulfil an individual child's needs; the processes, procedures and requirements before, during and after adoption are different. Various organisations are involved some statutory, others voluntary. Local authorities, national and local government, charities, family systems, pressure groups, courts, schools and health services are involved. "Adoption" is a hugely complex system and attempting to pinpoint specific areas affected by social networking is futile. Stepping back and looking at the big picture gives far more clarity because you, the reader, have specific expertise and knowledge in your operational area so can identify the factors most relevant to you. Metaphorically you can "join up your own dots" and ask your own "what if" questions to predict possible future scenarios and issues in your field.

Systems thinking is seeing beyond what appear to be isolated and independent incidents to deeper patterns. Looking at the big picture, the "adoption system" is a mass of national, regional and departmental systems in various organisations with differing structures, objectives, assessment procedures, rules, standards, regulations and operational practices: a maze of overlapping interrelated systems and heaps, where wheels move within bigger wheels. Impossible to define, so another model which offers the reader some distance from their own personal position and the opportunity to scan other horizons is useful.

Contingency model

The theoretical model below is used to understanding organisational behaviour. Based on the work of H. M. Carlisle, it is offers an approach which recognises that organisations have internal and external forces affecting them. The model can be applied in many areas and offers food for thought. Although "adoption" is not a specific organisation as such, applying this model can offer a different perspective on factors affecting adoption, particularly the external forces, which include social networking, political change and austerity measures. It also graphically demonstrates the interrelationship of the components and the need for systems thinking rather than trying to tackle various individual heaps.

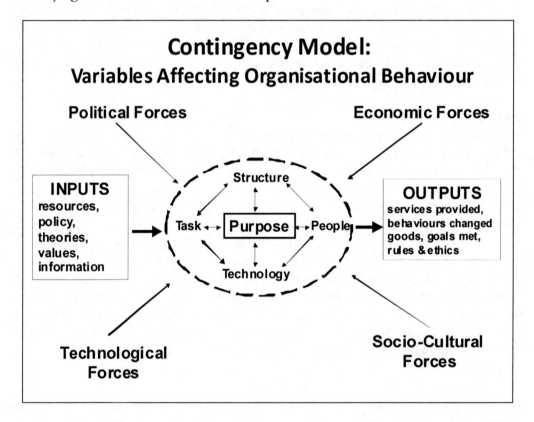

Remember models are never perfect or 'right', just helpful. The Contingency model can be applied widely as a method of noticing and acknowledging complex change. It can serve as a useful tool to diffuse the inevitable emotional reaction stemming from any organisational change. It can be applied to teams, local authorities, individual departments, schools and even individual families. For instance, just imagine which components are changed within a family when a baby is born. Pause. Now reflect how the components of that family system are affected when months or years later that child is removed.

The 'outputs' can be used to measure success, which might be customer satisfaction, targets met, evidence of goals achieved, maybe influencing, educating, healing or changing behaviours. Comparing output to purpose can sometimes reveal areas within an organisation which don't buy into that common purpose, because their perception of company purpose and values conflicts with their day to day existence. A classic example is organisations with mission statements which generate wry laughter in their staff.

Organisational External Variables	General Examples	Examples relating to Adoption
Political	Acts of parliament Legislation, Law reform Training for social workers, teachers, Rogue politicians Changes of Local or National Government	Adoption & Children Bill 2002 Social worker training Introduction of Special Guardianship Changes in regulations Serious Case reviews
Economic (Including all types of scarce resources)	Recession, inflation, resources, banking, financial constraints, budgets	Adoption support Funding for therapy LA budget constraints
Socio- Cultural	Changing values in society, attitudes, educational opportunities, Civil unrest, press and TV influences	No longer relinquished babies. Impact of drugs and alcohol on foetus and parenting capacity. Media campaigns
Technological	Scientific and technical advances and their applications. Growth of knowledge and innovations	Social Networking, Brain imaging, mobile phones. Teenagers much more knowledgeable than their parents. Information accessible anywhere anytime

Internal Organisational Variables	General Examples	Examples relating to adoption
Purpose	What does the organization do? Why does it exist? What business are we in?	Removing child from abusive and neglectful parents. Place child with approved, trained and supported adoptive parents.
Technology	Tools, equipment, hardware, software,	National adoption register for matching
Structure	Shape of organization, hierarchy, span of control, geographic location, decision making, integration, coordination, relationships, management, leadership	Possibility Changing Adoption Panels being run by individual Local Authorities to Regional Panels National Guidelines & Standards Adoption Parties
Task	Activities people engage in. Roles, responsibilities, assigned functions	Manage budgets, manage people, support others, lead, make policy, Completing CPR & other reports
People/players	Infinitely varied in age, sex, education, intellect, training, aspirations, values, motives, experience, beliefs, interests	Adoptive, birth and foster parents. Social workers. Various levels of decision makers, including Government Ministers, Judges, family support workers, Heads of Children's Services, Therapists

The old model

Facebook has shattered the existing adoption model, which assumes that the vast majority of adopted children will have no direct contact with their birth family until adulthood, and remain with their adoptive parents who will continue to be their 'main' set of parents in adulthood. The vast majority of adoption decisions including choice of placement, contact and support plans are based on this premise. Thanks to Facebook the birth family are unexpectedly back in the lives and faces of adopted children. That is now a fact. It will continue. Children being placed for adoption yesterday, today and tomorrow will be impacted by this technological advancement, and other inventions we can't yet imagine, envisage, dream or even fantasise about.

So an external technological force is shattering the current adoption model. However while the spotlight for the media and politicians is on the emotionally charged 'front end' of adoption, the placement of children: the later stages, the consequences of maltreatment, trauma and the challenge of parenting hurt children remains in the shadows. It's glaringly obvious that the spotlight's aperture must widen to incorporate the entire life span of the child.

Adoption as a lifelong issue and legacy of trauma

Adoption is a lifelong state. Loss, trauma, confusion, mixed messages, families with conflicting values, identity and heritage are all issues which cycle and resurface at different stages throughout an adoptees life. The complications during adolescence have been addressed earlier. However during mid childhood between about seven and nine, as cognitive thinking skills develop, fresh questions are raised, then in early adulthood intimate relationships, sex, and parenthood all bring extra questions, the revisiting of earlier beliefs and values and more curiosity. Medical and genetic questions raise another set of problems. The adoption process does not stop when a child is placed with a new family, but the media glare and public interest fixates on the "creation of a new family" stage. Neither want to hear about the trauma-triggered behaviour, sexual abuse disclosures, poor attention span or self-harming because it fails to sell newspapers. The legacy of trauma is the elephant in the living room.

We must step back, then back again yet another few steps to view the entire length of a child's life before making decisions. What do we want them to be doing or thinking when they are ten, fifteen, twenty, thirty or forty? What do they aspire to? What beliefs do they have about themselves and the world? Transformation takes time. The beliefs of an infant with the poor attachments listed in Chapter 2 will modify over time with therapeutic reparenting, appropriate therapy, good support at school and within the community. There are no quick fixes, but some strategies are better than others.

To inoculate children from sudden destabilising social networking contact and avoid surprises and explosions later, they must from an early age know the outline facts about their lives, the fundamental truth jigsaw pieces. This can only happen if we update the core principles of adoption, redesign the framework and structure within which they operate and change our mindset.

Back to basics: fundamental principles

Let's just for a moment ask ourselves: what do we want for maltreated children who can no longer live with their birth families? I think the answer includes:

Δ Permanent replacement adults who can offer a life time of stability, healing and security to a child

Δ Adults who can consistently therapeutically reparent the child, teenager and young adult

Δ A safe space to process the painful jigsaw pieces of their life history and to construct a coherent narrative which heals their pain and repairs their damaged psyche

Δ An environment which permits a maltreated child to develop an updated belief system, encouraging positive self-esteem, an internal working model

175

which integrates the past, provides robust internal resources and offers a hopeful, joyful, interesting, option-filled future

Δ A realistic view of their birth family which might include some well structured and meaningful contact

Δ A strong community which embraces the child and his "permanent parents"

Δ A cohort of legislators, educators, legal and social care professionals who "get" trauma

Permanent parents

Children need "permanent parents": parents with whom they will live until adulthood. Whether this is through the legal route of adoption, fostering, special guardianship or some other legal framework, is secondary to the need for true "permanence" i.e. the same home and nurturing adults for all their childhood and beyond.

Permanent parents of maltreated children need support, help, ongoing training and nurturing because for decades they live with and manage very difficult challenging behaviour.

The diagram gives a sense of the various sets of individuals and organisations needed to support parents who have to safely contain the child while the bubble wrap melts. Some will be involved with the child and family directly, others form part of the necessary infrastructure.

The diagram may look messy and rough round the edges, but it's an accurate reflection of the varying levels of intimacy required at different times by those who support each individual traumatised child; highlighting the complex nature of adoption and fostering.

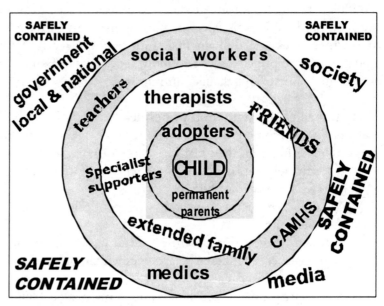

Please remember that even though this book has focused on adopted children, which is my primary knowledge base, many of the same principles, dilemmas, problems and challenges apply equally to children in local authority care (LAC), most of whom are fostered. The big issue is the legacy of trauma; the legal status is a minor factor.

Opportunity with new model and mindset shift

Any new model has to start from where we are, not where we wish we were. Massive redesigns, restructuring organisations, adding more or less layers of management, new standards, and codes of conduct or other structural adjustments may or may not be appropriate. I am certainly not offering or suggesting new structures or reorganisations, while these may occur, they are beyond the scope of this book.

I am suggesting a new mindset, one in which the legacy of trauma is fully spotlighted, acknowledged and these learnings integrated at every level, in every decision and throughout the entire system. My eight formal recommendations are listed in Part 4. If healing trauma becomes a core objective, the transformation of adoption will be positive.

A new mindset would add the following to existing adoption models and processes, easily fitting with some of the new ideas and proposals for changes in adoption practices being considered by central government.

Δ Ongoing access to high quality therapy for all adopted children from early childhood to early adulthood, so they can process 100% of the truth about their early life

Δ Ongoing robust support for adoptive families, before, during and after adoption

Δ Facilitated contact organised between the adopted child and birth parents using a skilled third party

Δ Recognition by all those who touch the lives of traumatised children that these children have complex needs which sometimes require counter intuitive management and strategies

Δ Independent support for birth parents

The last word

We have reached the end of our journey, you have a mixture of metaphors and models floating in your head, several partially completed jigsaws and hopefully both a curiosity to learn more and a desire to apply your new learnings to the life of at least one adopted or fostered child.

You can't step into the same river twice, so you may find that rereading the book, or dipping into some chapters again is useful. We did meander. Also as we established in Chapter 6, learning is an active process. For learning to occur you need to do something, reflect on it, draw conclusions, plan the next steps, then do something, reflect, theorise, plan, do, review, conclude and so on repeatedly. Revisiting any of the models and ideas in this book with your updated knowledge, will result in fresh perspectives and new unknowns.

Understanding and overcoming the legacy of childhood trauma is a fierce challenge for all involved and requires huge courage from all participants. It constitutes a major part of Making Sense of Nonsense, my next book.

Our desire must be that traumatised children learn new ways of being, thinking and behaving, build a solid sense of self and develop a more empowering belief system. Surely we as responsible adults should lead by example and face up to the truth that trauma pervades adoption. If we do, Facebook has done us a huge favour shattering the existing model. If we don't, adoption as we know it will die a slow death.

Do we have the courage to "get trauma"; modify our model, mindset and so transform adoption? I hope so.

> *"Courage is not the absence of fear but rather the judgement,*
> *that something else is more important than fear."*
> Ambrose Redmoon

PART 4: RECOMMENDATIONS

"It takes a village to raise a child,
a town to raise a challenging child and
an entire city to raise a traumatized child."
Helen Oakwater

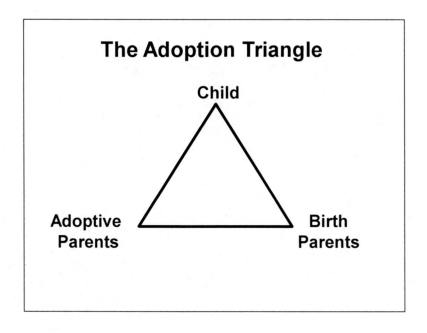

The Adoption Triangle

Child

Adoptive
Parents

Birth
Parents

CHAPTER TWENTY ONE

EIGHT RECOMMENDATIONS

1. Independent counselling for birth parents

Birth parents who have lost children to adoption need an independent counselling and support service. Currently the local authority involved with the removal of the child offers such support, which contaminates them in the eyes of the birth parent. This service could be regional or national, staffed by suitably trained counsellors, therapists or coaches, rather than social workers. Unjustly social workers are frequently perceived as perpetrators by birth parents and for interventions to be effective the client must trust their practitioner.

2. Provide cameras for police and social workers

Professionals should either be provided with specific cameras to record scenes or encouraged to take photographs with their mobile phones and facilities to down load the pictures in the office. This would be evidence for the child and invaluable for 100% truth life story work.

3. Speed up the entire adoption process: damage limitation

The drifts and delays within the UK adoption system are well known and systemic change is needed. This is currently being reviewed, so I will not address it here, but simply remind readers that drift and delay impacts the neuro-sequential development of the child. Delay increases the damage to the child and reduces the time for restorative therapeutic reparenting.

4. Improve adopter preparation and provide high quality ongoing training

Prospective adopters already receive training before they are approved. That should be compulsory between approval and the placement of their child and be accessible until the child reaches twenty-one. The culture of continuous learning and curiosity should pervade adoptive parenting. The technological advances in brain scanning and the developing knowledge in trauma resolution should be proactively shared with all adopters and foster carers.

5. Support adopters to reparent their children therapeutically

Δ   Adopters need continual, robust integrated support from the time of placement until the child is 21, from education, health and social services

Δ   Adopted children lose their LAC (Looked After Children) status and the accompanying 'privileges' when adopted. Due to their early experiences they are still children who 'LACk', hence should keep those educational, social and health benefits

Δ   Therapists who will work with the family to deliver 100% truth telling and organize facilitated contact during early, middle and late childhood and adolescence.

6. Educate therapists in trauma, trauma-triggered behaviour and a range of healing processes

Therapist working with adoptive families must understand the impact of infant maltreatment and trauma. Therapists working with adoptive and foster families must be trained in the resolution of trauma, the power of truth telling and how to facilitate effective, empowering contact.

7. Provision for facilitated contact

This is a tricky one, because face-to-face facilitated contact may not be a realistic objective for all participants, especially when unsupervised social media fulfils many of the superficial objectives for children and birth parents. However wherever possible it is the preferred route and should be encouraged, facilitated, with all corners of the adoption triangle being supported.

8. Invite Facebook to acknowledge the situation and offer significant funding for healing

While Facebook can't possibly be held responsible for how its members use their site, it can step up and recognise its corporate responsibility for the unintended consequences that social networking has reaped on adoption. Of course they didn't cause the problem, but they have the funds and technological knowhow to make a massive positive contribution to the adoption and fostering world, maybe by funding structured, facilitated contact.

The recommendations above result from my thinking and link purely to the content of Bubble Wrapped Children.

The following is the executive summary/key policy recommendations from Adoption UK's Supporting Adopters published in October 2011 which relate to wider issues in the adoption world and reproduced in full with kind permission. I agree with all the recommendations.

SUPPORTING ADOPTERS:
Published by Adoption UK October 2011

Educational issues for adopted children
Adopted children should have the same status as looked after children in relation to their educational need, including:
- Δ Priority in the school admissions systems.
- Δ Entitlements to additional support under the statementing system.

Recruitment of adoptive parents
- Δ Make recruiting adopters a national priority that is implemented nationally, rather than implemented locally, e.g, consider the possibility of a central recruitment agency for potential adopters who are unable to have their interest in adoption considered due to their local agencies exercising "local discretion" because they are only looking for adopters who can meet the needs of local children.
- Δ Positively and continuously promote adoption as a positive option.

Joint working
- Δ Better joint working between social services, education and health departments, focusing on providing improved adoption support services to families.

Children's needs to be central – early intervention
- Δ Departmental policy frameworks to put children's needs (as understood from a trauma perspective) at the centre of the decision-making process.
- Δ Using model of early intervention, based on a "child in need" approach, rather than child protection.
- Δ Early multi-agency support/intervention systems to be triggered at 20 weeks' gestation for "vulnerable parents" where one or more risk factors identified.
- Δ Ongoing multi-agency work support and intervention, both with those children identified in the womb, and those who come to the system's attention after birth or at a later age.
- Δ Greater use of concurrent planning and fewer moves for children in the care system.

The full report is at www.adoptionuk.org

BUBBLE WRAPPED CHILDREN

SELECTED BIBLIOGRAPHY

Archer C & A Burnell (ed) (2003) *Trauma, Attachment and Family Permanence.* Jessica Kingsley

Archer C & Gordon C (2006) *New Families, Old Scripts.* Jessica Kingsley

Archer C (1997) *First Steps in parenting the child who hurts.* Jessica Kingsley

Archer C (1999) *Next Steps in parenting the child who hurts.* Jessica Kingsley

Argent H (ed) (2003) *Models of Adoption Support.* BAAF

Baron-Cohen S (2011) *Zero Degrees of Empathy* Penguin

Barrett R (2006) *Building a Values Driven Organisation* Elisevier

Beesley P: (2011) Identifying Neglect. London BAAF

Berne E: Games People Play (1964)

Bradshaw J (1990) *Homecoming.* Piatkus

Brazelton T & Greenspan S (2000) *The Irreducible Needs of Children.* Perseus

Briere J (1992) *Child Abuse Trauma.* Newbury Park, London, New Delhi: Sage

Cairns K (2002) *Attachment trauma and Resilience.* BAAF

Charlton L, Crank M, Kansara K, Oliver C (1998). *Still screaming – Birth parents compulsorily separated from their children.* Manchester: After Adoption

Charvet SR (1995) *Words that Change Minds.* Dubuque Iowa: Kendall/Hunt

Dawson P & Guare R (2004) *Executive Skills in Children and Adolescents - A Practical Guide to assessment and Intervention.* Guildford Press

Department for Education and Science (2004) *Practice Guidance on Assessing the Support Needs of Adoptive Families.* HMSO

Department of Health (1999) *Adoption Now – Messages from Research.* John Wiley & Sons

Dilts R & DeLozier J (2000) *Encyclopaedia of systemic Neuro-Linguistic Programming and NLP New Coding.* Scotts Valley CA: NLP University Press

Dilts R (1990) *Changing Belief Systems with NLP.* Capitola CA: Meta publications

Dilts R (1994) *Strategies of Genius Volume 2.* Capitola CA: Meta Publications

Dilts R (1994) *Strategies of Genius Volume1.* Capitola CA: Meta Publications

BUBBLE WRAPPED CHILDREN

Dilts R (2003) *From Coach to Awakener.* Capitola: Meta Publications

Dilts R, Hallbom T & Smith S (1990) *Beliefs Pathways to Health and Wellbeing.* Portland: Metamorphous Press

Dwivedi K N (2000) *Post-Traumatic Stress Disorder in Children and Adolescents* Whurr

Faber A & Mazlish E (1980) *How to Talk so Kids will Listen and Listen so Kids will Talk* New York: Avon Books

Fahlberg V (1988) *The child in placement: common behavioural problems* BAAF

Fahlberg V (1991) *A child's journey through placement.* BAAF

Forward S (1989) *Toxic Parents* Bantam

Gallwey T (1975) *The Inner Game of Tennis.* London: Jonathan Cape Ltd

Gerhardt S (2004) *Why Love Matters – How affection shaped a baby's brain.* Hove & New York Brunner-Routledge

Gilligan S (1997) *The Courage to Love.* New York, London: W W Norton & Co

Goddard S (2002) *Reflexes, Learning and Behaviour – a Window into the Child's Mind* Oregon: Fern Ridge Press

Goddard S (2002) *Reflexes, Learning and Behaviour.* Fern Ridge Press

Goldman D (1998) *Working with Emotional Intelligence*

Grandin T (1995) *Thinking in Pictures and other reports from my life with Autism.* New York: Vintage Books/Random House

Grinder Michael: Group Mastery Certification Programme (unpublished)

GrinderM *(2004) Charisma The Art of Relationships* Michael Grinder& Associates

Haley J (1986) *Uncommon Therapy.* London, New York: WW Norton & Co

Hammond C (2005) *Emotional Rollercoaster* Harper Perennial

Hannaford C (1995) *Smart Moves* Great Ocean Publishers

HM Government, DCFS. "Working Together to Safeguard Children", published in 2010 by

Honey P & Mumford A (2006) The Learning Styles Questionnaire

Howe D & Feast J (2000) *Adoption, Search and Reunion.* London:The Children's Society

Howe D (1998) *Patterns of adoption* Blackwell Science

Howe D (2005) *Child Abuse and Neglect, Attachment Development and Intervention.* Basingstoke: Palgrave Macmillan

Hughes D (1997) *Facilitating Developmental Attachment.* Jason Aronson Inc

Hughes D (1998) *Building the Bonds of Attachment,* Northvale: New Jersey: London: Jason Aronson INC

James T & Woodsmall W (1988) *Time Line therapy and the Basis of Personality.* Capitola CA: Meta Publcations

Jewett C (1994) *Helping Children Cope with Separation and loss.* Batsford

Keck G & Kupecky R (1995) *Adopting the Hurt Child.* Pinon Press

Kranowitz C S (1998) *The Out-of-Sync Child* Perigee/Berkley

Kubler-Ross E (1981) *Living with Death and Dying.* London Souvenir Press

Levine P & Kline M (2007) *Trauma Through a Child's Eyes.* Berkeley, North Atlantic Books

Levine P (1997) *Waking the Tiger* North Atlantic Books

Levine P (2008) *Healing Trauma,* Boulder: Sounds True

Lewis T ((2000) *A General Theory of Love.* Random House

Lipton B (2005) *Biology of Beliefs.* Santa Rosa Mountain of Love/ Elite Books

Levy T & Orlans M (1998) *Attachment Trauma and Healing.* CWLA Press

Lowe N & Murch M (1999) *Supporting Adoption – Reframing the Approach.* BAAF

Loxterkamp L (2009) *Contact and Truth: The unfolding Predicament in Adoption and Fostering.* Clinical Child Psychology and Psychiatry, Sage Publications

Maguire Pavao J *The Family of Adoption* Boston: Beacon Press

McDermott I & Jago W (2001) *Brief NLP Therapy.* London: Sage Publications

McDermott I & Jago W (2001) *The NLP Coach.* London: Piatkus

McDermott I & O'Conner J (1996) *NLP & Health.* London: Thorson

Morgan N (2005) *Blame my Brain* London Walker Books

Morris A (1999) *The Adoption Experience.* London: Jessica Kingsley

Naparstek B (2006) *Invisible heroes – Survivors of trauma and how they heal.* New York London: Piatkus

BUBBLE WRAPPED CHILDREN

Neil E et al (2011) *Supporting Direct Contact after Adoption*, London: BAAF

O'Conner J & McDermott I (1997) *The Art of Systems Thinking*. Thorsons

O'Conner J & Seymour J (1994) *Training with NLP*. London: Thorsons

Perry B & Szalavitz M (2006) *The boy who was raised as a dog:* New York, Basic Books

Phillips R *Children exposed to parental substance misuse* London BAAF

Prior V 7 Glaser D (2006) *Understanding Attachment and attachment Disorders – Theory Evidence and Practice*. London: Philadelphia: Jessica Kingsley

Randolph E (2002) *Children who shock and surprise*. RFR publications

Read R & Burton K (2004) *Neuro-Linguistic Programming for Dummies*. Chichester: John Wiley & Sons

Rosen S (1982) *My Voice will go with you*. London, New York: WW Norton & Co

Schore A (2003) *Affect Regulation and the Repair of the Self* New York: WW Norton & Co

Seigel D (1999) *The Developing Mind*. Guildford Press

Siegel D & Hartzell M (2004) *Parenting from the Inside Out*. Penguin

Szalavitz M & Perry B (2010) *Born for Love*. New York Harper Collins

Tammet D (2006) *Born on a Blue day*. London: Hodder & Stoughton

Turnbull G (2011) *Trauma: From Lockerbie to 7/7: How trauma affects our minds and how we fight it:* Bantam Press

UK Government: *Adoption and Children Act 2002*

Van der Kolk B, McFarlane A, Weisaeth L (eds) (1996) *Traumatic Stress. The effects of Overwhelming Experience on Mind, Body and Society*. Guildford Press

Van Gulden & Bartels-Rabb L (1999) *Real Parents Real Children*. Crossroad

Verrier NN (1993) *The Primal Wound*. Baltimore: Gateway Press

Lightning Source UK Ltd.
Milton Keynes UK
UKOW041343060112

184839UK00001BA/35/P